D1622616

Power Up
Published by Orange, a division of The reThink Group, Inc.
5870 Charlotte Lane, Suite 300
Cumming, GA 30040 U.S.A.

The Orange logo is a registered trademark of The reThink Group, Inc.

Other Orange products are available online and direct from the publisher. Visit our website at www.WhatIsOrange.org for more resources like these.

ISBN: 978-1-63570-089-3
©2019 The reThink Group, Inc.

reThink Conceptual Team: Brandon O'Dell, Sarah Anderson, Ben Crawshaw, Mike Clear
Lead Writer: Lauren Terrell
Lead Editor: Melanie Williams
Editing Team: Mike Tiemann, Elloa Davis, Dan Scott, Molly Bell
Art Direction: Sharon VanRossum, Nate Brandt
Project Manager: Nate Brandt
Book Design, Layout, and Additional Illustration: Jacob Hunt

Printed in the United States of America
First Edition 2019
1 2 3 4 5 6 7 8 9 10

POWER UP

RAISE YOUR GAME

START HERE.

Oh, hey! I'm so glad you're here. Well, there. Wherever you are. I'm just glad you decided to pick up this book and start reading.

You're going to love this devotional.

Oh, yeah, this is a devotional. A devotional is a book that helps you get closer to God. If you read a little each day, you'll be a whole lot wiser in about nine weeks. Maybe you're thinking, "Closer to God? A whole lot wiser?? NINE weeks?! I thought this was a book of gaming tips." If that's what you're thinking, DON'T GO YET! It's *also* a book with gaming tips.

Pro Tip #1:

If you're too close to a creeper, don't be.

See? It can be both. A book to improve your gaming skills AND your life skills.

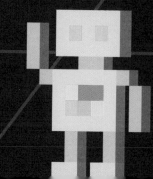

So let's start with the basics: why is this book called *Power Up*? Long story short, God made the earth. And when He did, He made people to be His good friends. But we sinned and messed it all up. We couldn't be close to God anymore—our hearts were stained by sin. But God didn't give up. He sent His Son, Jesus, to earth. Jesus lived a perfect life and died to take the punishment for all our sin so He could give us clean hearts and we could be close to God again.

> SIN is any thought, word, or action that breaks our relationship with God and others.

But that's not all of the story. Even though Jesus was killed, He *didn't stay dead*. Instead, He came back to life three days later and rose up to heaven some time after that. For real. People saw it and wrote about it in the Bible.

A short time after He disappeared behind the clouds, Jesus sent the Holy Spirit to be with us, inside us. Before you get all creeped out, this is actually pretty amazing.

The Holy Spirit is God Himself. He's God's very Spirit. So the Holy Spirit is God with you *all of the time*. Remember how God has always wanted to be close to people? The Holy Spirit living inside of you is God being closer than close. You can be the closest of friends with God! And what's also amazing is that He'll grow some pretty awesome stuff in your life. Check out how the Apostle Paul described it:

> But the fruit the Holy Spirit produces is love, joy and peace. It is being patient, kind and good. It is being faithful and gentle and having control of oneself.
>
> **Galatians 5:22-23a, NIrV**

When Jesus went back to heaven, He gave us the ultimate power boost. Because when we believe in Jesus, the Holy Spirit comes to live in us and to grow these things in us: **love, joy, peace, patience, kindness, goodness, faithfulness, gentleness,** and **self-control**. God's Spirit is so good, that's just what He grows in our hearts when we're close to Him.

You know how you get power ups in Mario Kart—things that make you better, stronger, more equipped to play the game? That's what each of those qualities of the fruit of God's Spirit is like. They're like **Power Ups**! They help us get stronger, better, and more equipped to handle whatever life throws our way. And the stronger our relationship is with Jesus, the easier it becomes to see those power ups in our lives.

So that's why the title of this book is *Power Up*! Whatever situation you're facing, the Holy Spirit is with you, and He can help you power up!

Now, think it over. Sleep on it. Run around Mario World a little. And when you're ready to learn how to grab onto God's Holy Spirit like a super-charged Mario star, turn to Week 1, Day 1 and get started!

Oh! And one more thing before you jump into the rest of this book: pick one adult you really like and trust. Maybe a parent, aunt, uncle, coach, or small group leader. Maybe the person who gave you this devotional. Tell that person you are starting to read this book. That you want to make it all the way through, but you might need their help. And one way they can help you

YOU WILL FIND THE MEMORY VERSE AT THE BEGINNING OF EACH WEEK.

(It's called the Memory Verse Challenge. Duh.)

Challenge your adult partner to memorize it. (You might even give them the memory verse cards at the end of this book to help them.) Check in on their progress through the week. Then, at the end of the week, sign off on whether your partner completed the challenge (whether they memorized the verse). Feel free to give them prizes for memorizing it. (Might we suggest: Doing extra chores for them or giving them a piece of candy from that secret stash under your mattress?)

And remember . . .

Pro Tip #2:

If there's a bottomless pit to your left, don't turn left. (You didn't think I'd forget the pro tips, did you?)

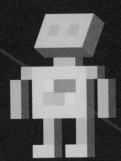

LEVEL ONE

WEEK 1

LOVE

We begin our 9-week journey with the "big one."

L-O-V-E

It may be the second smallest word (next to joy), but it is the biggest, heaviest, and juiciest part of the fruit of the Spirit.

Love changes everything. It changes how you treat others. It changes how you treat God. It changes how you treat yourself. Love can make you more joyful, peaceful, patient, kind, good, faithful, gentle—well, you get the picture. Love is really *the* most important part of the fruit of the Spirit.

So, let's start with love.

Define "love" in your own words:

Remember that memory verse thing we talked about a few pages ago? If not, flip back to page 7.

Here's this week's Memory Verse Challenge for the adult you picked. ★

> Love is patient, love is kind. It does not envy, it does not boast, it is not proud. It does not dishonor others, it is not self-seeking, it is not easily angered, it keeps no record of wrongs. Love does not delight in evil but rejoices with the truth. It always protects, always trusts, always hopes, always perseveres. Love never fails.
>
> **1 Corinthians 13:4-8a, NIV**

Pro Tip #3:

If you need directions and don't have a compass, look for the sun or stars. They always move toward the west. (Hey, that's a Minecraft pro tip and a life pro tip!)

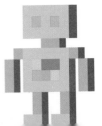

DAY 1

WHAT IS LOVE?
1 Corinthians 13:4-8a

The English language is weird. Take a minute and match the beginnings of these sayings to their endings. (If you need a little help with the answers, flip to page 15.)

Time flies when you're   the weather.

It's the best of   as good as mine.

So far   having fun.

I'm feeling under   so good.

Your guess is   pie.

It's as easy as   both worlds.

Have you ever heard the phrase "easier said than done"? It means that it's easier to *say* you'll keep your room clean for a month than actually keeping it clean. It's easier to tell a friend you'll meet them at the trampoline park than it is to convince someone to drive you there. It's easier to say you'll start going to bed earlier than to actually turn off the Nintendo Switch and close your eyes.

Pretty much everything in life is easier said than done (except maybe Peter Piper picked a peck of pickled peppers). That's especially true about love.

How many times do you think you've said you love something in the past week? Circle one:

Fewer than 5   5–10   10–20   More than 20

But saying you love something or someone and actually loving are two different things. Love (the kind of love described in the Bible, the kind of love Jesus said is most important, the very first part of the fruit of the Spirit) is easier said than done. In 1 Corinthians, we read:

> Love is patient, love is kind. It does not envy, it does not boast, it is not proud. It does not dishonor others, it is not self-seeking, it is not easily angered, it keeps no record of wrongs. Love does not delight in evil but rejoices with the truth. It always protects, always trusts, always hopes, always perseveres. Love never fails.
>
> **1 Corinthians 13:4-8a, NIV**

Not so easily done, right? You love your mom, but when she gets on the phone with Grandma, and all you need to know is what's for dinner, patience isn't easy. You love your best friend, but when you finally finish that 1,500-piece Minecraft LEGO set, the need to brag (or "boast") is hard to ignore. And then when your best friend buys the 3,000-piece Minecraft LEGO set, all you can think about is how much you want it.

Here's the thing that makes love so important: when you love well, the rest falls into place. When you love well, joy, peace, patience, kindness, goodness, faithfulness, gentleness, and self-control are a lot easier. So put love first, just like Jesus did. Put love first, just like Paul did when he wrote about the fruit (or power ups) of the Holy Spirit.

Go back and read 1 Corinthians 13:4-8a. Then think about how to show love (the 1 Corinthians kind of love) in the following situations. Write your ideas in the spaces below.

1. Your friend gets the thing you want most in the world:

2. Your little sister breaks the one thing you would save if your house were on fire:

3. You see one of your classmates being picked on by some older kids in your after-school program:

4. Someone on your soccer team thinks or believes something different from you:

Weird Sayings Answers:

Time flies when you're having fun.

It's the best of both worlds.

So far so good.

I'm feeling under the weather.

Your guess is as good as mine.

It's as easy as pie.

DAY 2

HOW DOES GOD SHOW LOVE?
John 3:16

Ding! Ding! Ding-ding-ding-ding-ding!

Mario flies across the screen, his legs pumping so fast, they look like a blur. He's farther than you've ever taken him. No star missed, the chime from each coin cheering him on, thumbs flying, Mario leaps over one, two, three lava pits, punches through a box, flattens himself against a wall, barely missing being smushed by a boulder. He quickly turns the corner into a boulder-free hallway. You've never been this close.

He falls between two walls. You didn't see it coming, but it's okay. You can get him out. All you have to do is leap, turn, leap, turn, leap—and he's back! Sprinting down the hall toward the floating lift that will finally take him to—**suddenly the screen goes black**. You frantically push buttons, move joysticks, jump to your feet, and that's when you see her. Your little sister holding the unplugged cord of the Nintendo Switch. She's laughing so hard she can't breathe.

You sit back down, heartbroken. You close your eyes and take a deep breath. Then you grab the second remote and hand it to her. You say, "Want to play? I could show you my favorite levels."

On a scale of 1 to 10, how likely is it that you would respond that way in that situation? Circle one:

Yeah, right.   Absolutely!
1 — 2 — 3 — 4 — 5 — 6 — 7 — 8 — 9 — 10

Most likely, you circled 1. Maybe if you're a really, really loving person you circled 2 or 3. If we are honest, it's hard to love someone who hurt us. But that's exactly what God did (and still does!).

Remember the story of Adam and Eve? They were the first humans God created. Everything was good; God said so Himself. There was light and oceans and animals and humans. It was like heaven on earth. Then Adam and Eve sinned. And then every single human after them kept on sinning and sinning and sinning.

God was hurt—really hurt. But He showed love in a really big, God-sized way. He sent Jesus. Why? Check out what John (one of Jesus' close friends) said:

> God so loved the world that he gave his one and only Son. Anyone who believes in him will not die but will have eternal life.
>
> **John 3:16, NIrV**

God sent Jesus to fix what we broke.

God sent Jesus to give us something we don't deserve: **eternal life**.

ETERNAL LIFE means life forever with God.

God sent Jesus because He loves us.

God could have gotten angry. He could have sent a boulder to smush Adam and Eve flat. He could have done nothing and just let us all die. The end. He could have said, "Oh, well. You deserve it."

But He didn't. He saved us by sending Jesus to pay for our sin, to die in our place, and to give us clean hearts. Because He loves us. And that's not all. After Jesus went to heaven, He sent the Holy Spirit to be with us.

So now YOU can have God-sized love. You have the ability to show others God's really, really BIG love. (Which must be why you didn't smush your sister for ruining your Mario game.)

On a scale of 1 to 10, how does it feel to know that the God who made everything loves you in such a big way?

Meh.   W-O-W!

1 — 2 — 3 — 4 — 5 — 6 — 7 — 8 — 9 — 10

Take a minute to talk to God. Close your eyes, write a prayer, or go for a walk so you can talk to Him out loud. Whatever feels most comfortable. He hears you no matter how you pray. If any questions or feelings come up while you're praying, talk to an adult (maybe the one who's working on memorizing those 1 Corinthians verses about love). ★

DAY 3

HOW CAN LOVE POWER UP MY LIFE?
1 Peter 4:8

Have you ever used the instant health potion in Minecraft?

1 water bottle
+ a little nether wart
+ a glistening melon =
health no zombie can touch

Did you know you can turn that potion into a splash potion? A potion you can throw at someone else to give them extra bars of health?

(I think we can call those Pro Tips #4 and #5.)

In real life, just like in Minecraft, we mess up. Instead of zombies and skeletons and creepers, we make bad decisions. We lie to someone, take more than our share, or a million other selfish things that make us (and others) feel **icky**.

> **icky (adj.):**
>
> **1.** That feeling you get in your stomach when you hope your friend never finds out you told his deepest, darkest secret.
>
> **2.** That feeling you get in your chest and stomach when your very best friend tells everyone your deepest, darkest secret.

But guess what? There's a real-life power up to take that icky feeling away, just like an instant health potion. Can you guess what it is?

LOVE!

In the Bible, Peter (one of Jesus' closest friends) told us:

> Most of all, love one another deeply.
> Love erases many sins by forgiving them.
>
> **1 Peter 4:8, NIrV**

Wow. Love can erase sin's ickiness with forgiveness. And no one knew this better than Peter. When Jesus was arrested and about to be killed, Peter ran and hid. He told people he'd never met that Jesus guy before. But when it turned out Jesus really was who He said He was, Peter felt really icky. He'd denied even knowing his best Friend.

But Peter didn't have to feel icky for long. Jesus showed Peter really big, God-sized love by forgiving him. It was like Peter's sin against God was erased. Ickiness gone. Health restored.

Peter + Jesus = BFFE

You can do the same thing. Love can help you forgive. When you love others (and God, and yourself), it's like having endless amounts of health potion to splash around in. People will still mess up. You will still mess up. (You will sin, even.) But the Holy Spirit can power you up with love to erase the ickiness of sin.

Flip back to Day 1 of this week and read 1 Corinthians 13:4-8a again. Is there a time you can think of when you didn't show that kind of love? Or when someone hurt you by not loving you in those ways? Draw what happened (in pencil) in the box below. Then, erase your picture and draw over it with a better choice—with how you could use the power of love to set things right.

LOOK OUT!

A hazard to love is pride.
(Hazard = danger or risk)

In Minecraft you have to look out for zombies, skeletons, and creepers. In real life, the stuff you have to look out for can be a lot harder to see. Love means thinking of others first. It means playing what your friend wants to play. It means sharing your favorite things, listening, caring, helping, and forgiving.

And none of that is possible when you are filled with pride. A little pride is okay. Like feeling good about something you worked really hard on.

But when you are so full of pride that you can't love others well, that's not good. That's when pride turns into a hazard and takes away your ability to love.

DAY 4

HOW DID PEOPLE IN THE BIBLE SHOW LOVE?
Luke 19:1-10

According to your parents, what do you think would be the worst thing you could be when you grow up?

Circle all that apply:

a lawyer

a politician

an acrobat

a tax collector

unhappy

Hopefully you circled "unhappy," and you know you have your parents' loving support no matter what career you choose. But that's not always the case. And it certainly wasn't the case in Jesus' day.

In Jesus' day, one of the worst things you could grow up to be was a tax collector. They were known for lying, for tricking people, and stealing their money. Sure, they were super-rich but they didn't have many friends. Even tax collectors didn't like tax collectors. No one wanted to be anywhere near them. Kind of like those little ghosts chasing Pac-Man.

Pro Tip #6:
**Your Pac-Man will never be eaten by
a ghost if you never play Pac-Man.**

But as you probably already know, Jesus loves everyone. When He was on earth, He loved tax collectors as much as He loved fishermen. He loved servants as much as kings. The only reason Jesus had for loving someone was: they were a *someone*.

In the book of Luke, chapter 19, there is a story about Jesus going to Jericho (JER-ih-koh). There was a super-rich and greedy tax collector named Zacchaeus (za-KEE-uhs) in Jericho. Zacchaeus climbed up in a tree to get a good look at this Jesus guy he'd heard so much about. Pretty much the whole town hated Zacchaeus. So when Jesus called out to Zacchaeus and asked if He could have lunch with him, everyone was shocked. Why would Jesus want to be around a person like that?

But Jesus didn't see Zacchaeus as a person like that. He didn't feel like He had to avoid Zacchaeus like a deadly Pac-Man ghost. When Jesus saw Zacchaeus, He saw someone to love. Someone who sinned and maybe who didn't quite fit in, but most importantly, *someone*.

Jesus wants you to love the same way. He wants you to see every person as a person to love. He wants you to love the people who are easy to love and the people who are hard to love. He wants you to love others not just because they are people you like, but because they are *people*. And the closer you get to Jesus, the more the Holy Spirit powers up your life, the easier it will be to love everyone.

Open your Bible or Bible app, and read Luke 19:1-10.

1. Why do you think Jesus chose Zacchaeus over everyone else in the crowd? (Hint: Read verse 10.)

   a. Zacchaeus had really cool sandals.

   b. Zacchaeus made a really great fish taco.

   c. People like Zacchaeus are the reason Jesus came to earth.

2. Why is it important to show love to the people everyone avoids?

   a. Everyone needs to be loved.

   b. Love has the power to change someone's whole life.

   c. All of the above.

3. How did Jesus' love change Zacchaeus?

   a. Zacchaeus' fish tacos + Jesus' recipe for the perfect chipotle mayo = perfection.

   b. Jesus' kindness made Zacchaeus want to be a better person.

   c. Zacchaeus was terrified of what Jesus might do to him if he sinned again.

4. How would your life be different if you showed love to everyone just because they are someone?

a. You would have a lot more friends.

b. A couple friends might start treating you differently.

c. You would spend less time trying to figure out who to like and who to avoid.

d. You would worry less about who liked you and why.

e. All of the above (and more).

DAY 5

POWER UP
1 JOHN 3:18

Do you know what a homograph is? It's a word with two or more meanings. Words like **bat**, **tear**, **wave**, **bow**, and **floss** are homographs.

> **Can you think of more than one meaning for all those words?**

Love is kind of like a homograph, too. You may *love* LEGO and Roblox and slime and your new Nikes. But not the same way you love Nana and Aunt Alma and Coach Rob and your best friend. How do you think those two loves are different?

Love is a feeling. A strong feeling. And just like sadness makes us cry and anger makes us stomp and joy makes us laugh, love makes us want to do something. What kinds of things does love make you want to do? Circle all that apply:

Write a song.   Help out.

Draw a picture.   Write a letter.

Talk for hours.   Say encouraging words.

Spend time together.   Do extra chores.

Buy them gifts.   Play games together.

Make cookies.   Give a pat on the back.

Tell inside jokes.   Give a high five.

Give a hug.   Shout from the rooftop.

Whether it's love for the cooking channel or for your grandma, love comes with an action. The only problem is, it's a lot easier to binge watch your favorite cooking show than to call your grandma. It's a lot easier to spend your entire Saturday reading (and loving) Harry Potter than to spend it playing with your little brother.

The love described in the Bible (the love that is the fruit of God's Holy Spirit) is the people kind of love. And the actions that come with loving people require you to put others first. That's why it's harder to love your brother than it is to love a good book.

> **Dear children, don't just talk about love. Put your love into action. Then it will truly be love.**
>
> **1 John 3:18, NIrV**

Read that last part again. The part that says, "Then it will truly be love." The thing that makes our love for others real is our actions. It's the only way the people we love will really feel our love. So while it might mean giving up something you really want (like the last piece of cake), loving others with your actions is so, so important.

Take a minute and make a list of the top five to ten people you love the most.

TOP PEOPLE

1
2
3
4
5
6
7
8
9
10

Now, think about each of those people and write the best way to show your love to that person. Maybe it's a phone call. Or a drawing. Maybe it's helping with the chores or sharing your candy. Maybe it's different for each person. (Hint: It's probably different for each person.)

So take a minute and really think about what is most important to that person. Then, put your love into action. ★

WAY TO SHOW LOVE

POWER UP CHALLENGE

You did it! You made it through the first week of devotionals!

First things first: Did your adult devotional partner memorize 1 Corinthians 13:4-8a?

☐ YES   ☐ NO

X _____

(sign your name here)

Bonus: What did you give them for memorizing the verse?

_____

Now for your own personal Power Up Challenge. Remember those names you wrote down yesterday? The top five to ten people you love most in your life? You're going to show them some love!

On the next page there are some love notes. WAIT! Before you get all grossed out about sending a love note to your grandma—or even worse, your brother—it's not that kind of love note. These are notes you can decorate and fill in however you want. Just write one reason you love that person (from the list you made yesterday).

Your challenge is to fill out (and deliver!) one note per person from your list. If you don't feel like using these notes, feel weird about cutting out a page from this awesome book, or just want an excuse to use your new art supplies, feel free to make your own. Just be sure to include one reason you really love that person. Then, deliver the notes through the mail (don't forget envelopes, addresses, and stamps) or in person.

Dear _____,

You are one of my favorite people on the planet. Why, you ask?

Because _____

_____

I really do love you tons. Love,

_____

Dear _____,

You are one of my favorite people on the planet. Why, you ask?

Because _____

_____

I really do love you tons. Love,

_____

Dear _____,

You are one of my favorite people on the planet. Why, you ask?

Because _____

_____

I really do love you tons. Love,

_____

Dear _____,

You are one of my favorite people on the planet. Why, you ask?

Because _____

_____

I really do love you tons. Love,

_____

Dear _____,

You are one of my favorite people on the planet. Why, you ask?

Because _____

_____

I really do love you tons. Love,

_____

Dear _____,

You are one of my favorite people on the planet. Why, you ask?

Because _____

_____

I really do love you tons. Love,

_____

Dear _____,

You are one of my favorite people on the planet. Why, you ask?

Because _____

_____

I really do love you tons. Love,

_____

Dear _____,

You are one of my favorite people on the planet. Why, you ask?

Because _____

_____

I really do love you tons. Love,

_____

Dear _____,

You are one of my favorite people on the planet. Why, you ask?

Because _____

_____

I really do love you tons. Love,

_____

Dear _____,

You are one of my favorite people on the planet. Why, you ask?

Because _____

_____

I really do love you tons. Love,

_____

LEVEL TWO

WEEK 2

JOY

Joy is more than laughing with friends over a massive ice cream sundae. It's deeper than smiling for family photos. It's bigger than winning your soccer tournament.

Life isn't all sundaes and smiles and trophies. Sometimes life feels a lot less . . . joyful. So that's when God's joy, the joy from the Holy Spirit, steps in.

The fruit-of-the-Spirit kind of joy is always possible, even when things aren't going your way. This kind of joy means knowing everything will be okay. It means making a choice to go looking for joy when all you really want to do is stomp on someone's foot.

What do you think true joy is?

Keep reading this week to find out if you're right!

Oh, and here's this week's Memory Verse Challenge. Don't forget to tell your partner! ★

> Always be joyful. Never stop praying.
> Give thanks no matter what happens.
>
> **1 Thessalonians 5:16-18a, NIrV**

Pro Tip #7:

If things aren't going your way while playing Minecraft, don't throw the screen across the room. Things only get worse from there.

DAY 1

WHAT IS JOY?
Philippians 4:4

Put a smiley face next to the things that make you happy:

	Brand-new shoes
	Mario falling into a bottomless pit
	New video games
	Cleaning your room
	People fighting at home
	All the slime in the world
	Getting in trouble at school
	A trip to Disney World
	A day at a trampoline park
	Failing a test
	Moving to a new town
	Your sister leaving for college
	Lifetime supply of bubble gum
	Raw veggies for dinner
	What you see and hear on the news
	Rainy days
	Unlimited screen time

Some of those things are easy to get excited about. New games? Unlimited screen time? All the slime?! Yes, please!

But joy isn't about being happy when things are going your way. Real, true joy means finding a way to be happy even when things *aren't* going your way. Like being happy even when you want a snack and all you have in your house is raw broccoli. Being happy even when you fail a test you studied really hard for. Being happy even when you see really scary stuff on the news.

Real joy doesn't always just bubble up inside you. Sometimes you have to look for it.

In the Bible, the Apostle Paul wrote:

CHECK OUT PAUL!

- √ also known as Saul
- √ used to hate Christians
- √ blinded by God
- √ started Christian churches all over the place
- √ went to jail and was killed for telling people about Jesus

> Always be joyful because you belong to the Lord. I will say it again. Be joyful!
>
> **Philippians 4:4, NIrV**

You see that first word? "Always". Paul really meant it. He knew what it meant to be joyful when you are in jail. To be joyful when people hate you. To be joyful when you don't have food or water or a place to sleep. He knew that all kinds of bad things can happen in life. But if your joy only comes from new toys, candy, and birthday parties, you will have a pretty joy-less life.

Where should joy come from? Re-read Paul's words (on page 43) and fill in the blanks to get the answer:

I BEL_____ G TO _____ H_L_____ D.

Real joy, the fruit-of-the-Spirit kind of joy, comes from knowing that you belong to God, that God loves you, and that God is with you no matter what happens.

> **DISAPPOINTED means feeling let down.**

Real joy doesn't mean you will never feel **disappointed**. That's impossible. So start by practicing real joy—looking for and finding a way to be happy. Then it will get easier and easier to get past disappointment and know you'll be okay . . . maybe even happy!

Take a minute and practice finding joy now. The first line is filled in for you as an example.

List three things that steal your joy	List three great things you always have
When my big brother is mean	God's love

Now, put those two lists together by completing these three sentences:

Even when _my big brother is mean_ , I can have joy

because I have _God's love_ .

Even when _____ , I can have joy

because I have _____ .

Even when _____ , I can have joy

because I have _____ .

Even when _____ , I can have joy

because I have _____ . ★

Pro Tip #8:

If you're having trouble finding joy, take a break. Stand on your head, or play a little Pokémon.

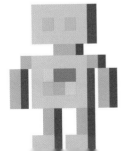

DAY 2

HOW DOES GOD SHOW JOY?
Zephaniah 3:17

Have you ever made something? Of course you have! You're a really smart, artistic, creative kid. Maybe you've made a robot, crunchy slime, a Minecraft mountain cave out of LEGO, or a perfectly delicious pineapple upside-down cake.

Draw a picture here of your favorite thing to make:

Have you ever made something that didn't turn out exactly as you hoped? Maybe your slime was a little too slimy. Or the spider-spawner on the side of your mountain cave would't rotate the way it's supposed to. Maybe your pineapple upside-down cake was more like pineapple upside-down mush.

Think for a minute about how you felt when things didn't turn out quite right. Did you still tell everyone about what you'd made? Did you enjoy showing it off, or were you embarrassed that it wasn't perfect?

God made you in His image. That means He made you to be like Him. God is creative, so He made you creative. God is wise, so He made you able to make wise choices. God loves, so He made you able to love.

However, you are not *exactly* like God: you aren't perfect. We all make bad choices. We don't love everyone all the time. We all do things that are wrong. But how do you think God feels about His not-so-perfect creations? Check out this verse from Zephaniah (zeh-fuh-NYE-uh):

> The Lord your God is with you. He is the Mighty Warrior who saves. He will take great delight in you. In his love he will no longer punish you. Instead, he will sing for joy because of you.
>
> **Zephaniah 3:17, NIrV**

Even though you aren't perfect, God takes delight in you. He will sing for joy because of you. (I like to imagine God doing The Worm to that "Everything Is Awesome" song when He thinks of me. But that may just be me.)

The point is, you make God happy because He made you and He loves you. His joy doesn't depend on what you do. Yes, He likes the way you put others first (most of the time). He is glad about how hard you worked on your last school project. But He also thinks of those hilarious jokes you tell and that one freckle Aunt Alma just can't stop pinching. God sees those things and takes delight.

God sets the example for how to be joyful. He wants us to take delight and rejoice in life.

In the space below, write or draw the song or dance you imagine God might do when He delights in you. ★

DAY 3

HOW CAN JOY POWER UP MY LIFE?
Nehemiah 8:10e

Have you ever heard the phrase "laughter is the best medicine"? It may not be true in every situation. (After all, if you have strep throat, you really do need antibiotics.) Still, study after study shows that being happy can actually help you live longer.

Scientists have found that being happy means you . . .

are less likely to get sick.
won't be as stressed out.
will be happier.

Okay, that last one is obvious. Being happy makes you happy. But isn't it wild that joy can actually affect things like heart disease and how long you live?

Talk about powering up!

But before we even knew what stuff like heart disease was, humans knew the power of joy. In the Bible, a man named Nehemiah once said:

> The joy of the Lord makes you strong.
>
> **Nehemiah 8:10e, NIrV**

What makes you strong? *The joy of the Lord.* Not just the happiness you get from a day spent building out your Minecraft world or the ultimate laser tag tournament. The joy that comes from God makes you *strong* because His joy is steady. It is constant, no matter what is going on. And did I mention it makes you strong?

When you get in trouble with your parents,
when your best friend hurts your feelings,
when you lose screen time for a whole week,
the joy of the Lord makes you strong.

That doesn't mean you'll never be sad (even though God's Spirit is with you). You will get sad, angry, hurt, and frustrated sometimes. But with the help of the Holy Spirit, those feelings won't keep you down long. You'll be able to get back up, to feel better sooner, and to find joy in all situations. He will help you power up!

Have you ever been able to be joyful when things weren't going your way? Draw a cartoon about that time here. ★

Next time things aren't going your way, ask God for His joy to make you strong.

LOOK OUT!
A hazard to joy is jealousy.

You know those guys that squirt ink on your screen in Mario Kart? You've got your eye on the finish line, and then all of a sudden all you can see are black spots and you fall off into darkness. Well, jealousy is kind of like those ink spots. When you focus on what other people have, you can't see all that you have to be grateful for. And that's when you fall into the bottomless pit of jealousy and totally miss out on JOY.

DAY 4

HOW DID PEOPLE IN THE BIBLE SHOW JOY?
Acts 16:16-40

Put the following in order from 1 to 5.

1 = easy to find a way to be happy
5 = never finding happiness no matter how hard I look

___ Pop quiz on the last day of school before summer break

___ Being beaten and thrown in jail for doing the right thing

___ A candy shop where everything is FREE

___ Losing the championship game

___ Having a sleepover with your best friend

PAUL and SILAS were two of the men who went around telling others that Jesus had risen from the dead and was really, truly, no lie, the Son of God.

Paul and **Silas** found themselves in one of those situations. Can you guess which one?

(If you guessed a free candy shop, guess again.)

Paul and Silas were in Philippi telling people about Jesus when they were arrested, beaten, and put in jail. In those days, the people in power were afraid of people thinking this Jesus guy was more powerful than they were.

They were afraid that if people believed Jesus really is the Son of God and started to follow Him, people wouldn't follow them anymore.

So when Paul and Silas started spreading the good news about Jesus and what He had done, the people in charge arrested the two men before things got out of hand. (Read Acts 16:16-40 if you want the whole scoop.)

Paul and Silas were doing exactly what God wanted them to do, but they got punished for it. They didn't know what would happen next. Would they be in a Philippian jail for weeks? Months? Years? Would they be beaten again? Starved? Put to death?

But they didn't let the fear of the unknown steal their joy. They didn't grumble and complain and give up.

While they were in jail, Paul and Silas prayed and sang songs. They were probably super-scared and confused. But they still turned to God. They found a way to be happy even when things were not going their way.

How would you feel if you were sitting in a smelly, uncomfortable, scary jail cell for doing the right thing? Would you feel like singing? Probably not. My guess is, Paul and Silas didn't feel like singing either. But they did it anyway. And I'd also guess it ended up making them feel a little more joyful. That's just the way joyful songs work.

Music is one of the best ways to find joy—singing, dancing, even playing an instrument if you can. Take a few minutes to sing, dance, or make some music. Find a place where you can be alone and *loud*, pick out a couple of songs that make you happy, and really get into them. Then, write the song titles you totally rocked on a notecard. Put the notecard in your backpack or tape it to a place you will see often. Dance, sing, or play those songs next time you're in need of a little joy! ★

DAY 5

POWER UP
1 Thessalonians 5:16-18a

Something to think about:

You can't have joy without gratitude.

There have been a lot of studies in the last few years about the importance of being grateful. In one of the more famous studies, scientists put a bunch of people into three different groups.

1	2	3
They told the first group of people to make a list of things they were grateful for each night before bed.	They told the second group to list things that happened that day that weren't good or bad.	They told the third group to list all the bad things that happened that day.

After a few weeks of doing this, the scientists asked each group how they were feeling. And they found that one of the groups was way happier and felt really good about life. Their friends and family even noticed they were in a better mood and much more fun to be around.

Which group do you think it was?

Yep! The group who thought about and wrote down all the things they were grateful for each day. (See? I told you you were smart.)

It probably doesn't take a group of super-genius scientists to figure out that when you think about all the good things, you're going to be a lot happier. In fact, Paul (not a super-genius scientist, but still really smart) put joy and gratitude together thousands of years ago:

> **Always be joyful. Never stop praying.**
> **Give thanks no matter what happens.**
>
> **1 Thessalonians 5:16-18a, NIrV**

Paul knew that when he prayed and gave thanks, he would be a lot happier (even if he was sitting next to his buddy in a dark, smelly Philippian jail).

And now, thousands of years later, scientists are proving that very thing:

GRATITUDE = JOY

Now it's your turn! Put a journal, notebook, or stack of scrap paper and a pen by your pillow. **For the next week, write at least three things you are grateful for each night before bed.** It can be the same three things every single night, but it'll work better if you find new things from your day. Then, as you fall asleep, think about those things. Soon, you'll be looking for things you can write down at the end of the day—things to be grateful for—instead of focusing on the bad. And then you will find it much easier to be joyful—no matter what.

Start here. Write three things you are grateful for. ★

1. _____

2. _____

3. _____

POWER UP CHALLENGE

Two weeks in and you already know a lot more about the Holy Spirit and two things He produces in us:

√ LOVE
√ JOY

But first things first: Did your adult devotional partner memorize 1 Thessalonians 5:16-18a?

☐ YES   ☐ NO

X _____

(sign your name here)

Bonus: What did you give them for memorizing the verse?

And now for your own personal Power Up Challenge:

Make
a
Joy Jar.

Materials:

1 (empty and cleaned out) jar with a lid*
1 piece of paper
Marker(s)
Scissors
Tape
All the decorations (optional)

*Can be an old peanut butter jar, salsa jar, Mason jar, or any empty jar you can find with a lid.

Instructions:

Start by decorating your Joy Jar. Use your piece of paper, marker(s), scissors, and tape to cover the original label with one that says "Joy Jar." Decorate your label however you want.

On the next page, you will see strips of paper that you can cut out (or you can make your own). Most of the ideas are written for you, but a few are left blank. Think of a few ways you can be happy when things aren't going your way. Write those ideas on the blank strips. Cut the strips apart, fold them, and put them in your Joy Jar.

The next time you get in trouble, feel angry, or feel sad, go to your Joy Jar. Pull out a strip of paper and do what it says. Some of the ideas may seem strange, but give them a try. You may be surprised how much easier it is to find joy afterward. ★

Run around your house or apartment building three times.

Blast your favorite music and dance alone in your room.

Scream as loud as you can into your pillow.

Go outside and jump as high as you can, as many times as you can.

Throw a (soft) ball against a wall.

Think of three things you are grateful for and say them out loud.

Take five deep breaths.

Pray and ask God to help you feel joy.

Run in place for 60 seconds.

Say "God loves me ALWAYS" out loud five times.

Get some sleep!

LEVEL THREE

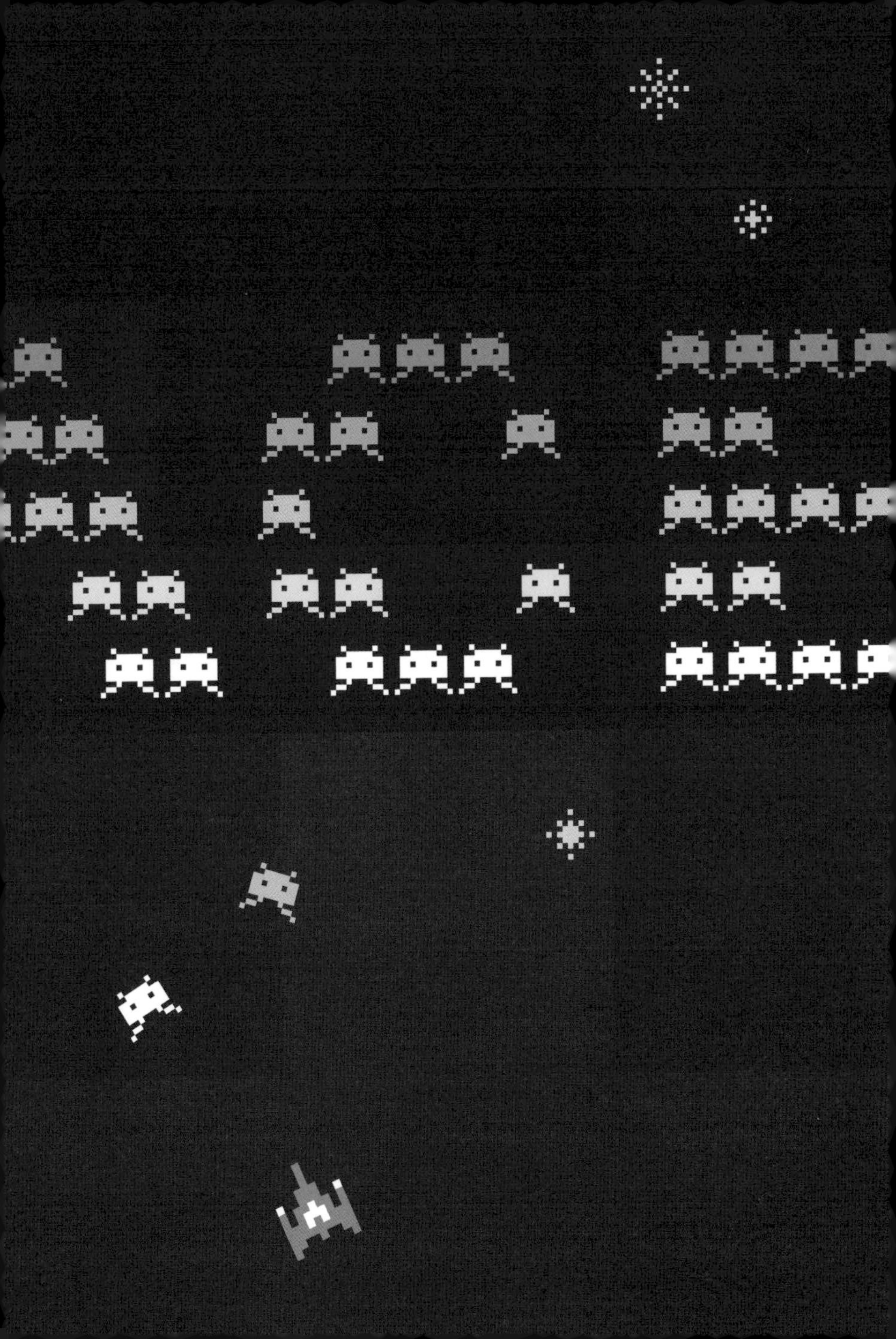

WEEK 3

PEACE

Peace. It's not just boring silence . . . never fighting . . . brushing things off, cool as a cucumber, when you're boiling over inside.

True peace comes from the Holy Spirit. What do you think that looks and feels like?

_____

_____

_____

_____

_____

_____

_____

The peace that comes from the Holy Spirit is always there. You can find it all alone in your backyard on a sunny day. You can find it when you're lost in the middle of a huge crowd. You can find it when everything is going your way. You can find it when peace seems like the last thing you should be feeling.

Keep reading if you could use some more of that kind of peace!

But before you turn the page, here's your new **Memory Verse Challenge**. Don't forget to challenge your partner to memorize it! Just think: it's a lot easier for you to have God's peace when the adults around you have it, too, #amiright? ★

Don't worry about anything; instead, pray about everything. Tell God what you need, and thank him for all he has done.

Philippians 4:6, NLT

DAY 1

WHAT IS PEACE?
Philippians 4:6-7

Wait! Before you get too cozy, find a quiet place to read this. Maybe it's your room or the bathroom. Or maybe you share your room with your hyper twin brothers and your dad has taken over your bathroom for the next 45 minutes. In that case, go outside. Or sit in a closet with the door closed. Wherever your quiet place is, go there now. I'll wait.

You there? Great! Now, set this book on your lap and sit in silence for two minutes. (Bonus points if you actually have a timer you can set.)

When you're done, write what you thought about and how it felt in the bubble above. Be honest!

Now try to sit in silence again for two more minutes. This time, get in a really comfy position. Take four super-deep and slow breaths. Close your eyes and imagine you are somewhere really peaceful. You get to pick the place! It can be somewhere real, like a beach, or somewhere you can only go in your imagination (like floating on a cloud). Spend two minutes focusing on that place. Think about what it feels like, smells like, looks like, and sounds like.

When you're done, write about how your body felt. Did you feel any different than you did during the first two minutes?

_____

_____

_____

_____

_____

Our brains are super-powerful. They can think a hundred different things almost at once. That can be useful, but not very peaceful, especially when half of those things are worries. _What's for dinner? Is that test today? Does my breath stink? Where did I put my left shoe? Is my hamster getting sick? How close is that hurricane I heard about in the news? Something smells like broccoli. Wait, what's for dinner?_

But when you focus your brain on something bigger than all of that, you feel more peace. Check out what Paul wrote in the book of Philippians:

> Don't worry about anything; instead, pray about everything. Tell God what you need, and thank him for all he has done. Then you will experience God's peace, which exceeds anything we can understand. His peace will guard your hearts and minds as you live in Christ Jesus.
>
> **Philippians 4:6-7, NLT**

God's peace sounds pretty nice, right? And that verse tells us how to get it. **Can you find the four ways the verse tells us we can experience God's peace?**

1 _____

2 _____

3 _____

4 _____

Don't worry about anything. Pray about everything. Tell God what you need. But most importantly, thank Him for all He has already done for you.

When you spend time with God every day, the peace of His Holy Spirit will come. The kind of peace that is there when things are smooth and when things get rough. The kind of peace that doesn't make any sense. The kind of peace you feel when you would normally freak out. The kind of peace that seems to happen for no reason at all.

How about practicing it now? Remember that peaceful place you pictured in your imagination? Close your eyes and go there again, but this time, imagine you are there with God. Picture Him there, sitting right next to you. Whenever you have a thought, whether it's gratitude, worry, or just plain wonder, imagine passing it over to God and going back to sitting in silence. With God's peace. ★

DAY 2

HOW DOES GOD SHOW PEACE?
Mark 4:35-41

Picture this: Your homework is done and your laundry is neatly folded and put away. There's an hour left before dinner, so you use a little of your screen time to play a game. Not long after you log on, storm clouds start to form on your screen. You know if you do nothing, your game will be over pretty soon. So you focus on:

[Circle one]

a that huge cyclone coming toward you and panic!

b making your way to the blue skies of the safe zone.

You probably chose option B. In a video game, it's easy to keep a level head and seek shelter or safety from a storm.

> ## Pro Tip #9:
> If you get caught in a video game storm, it doesn't help to put on your real-life rain boots.

But when real-life storms hit, it can feel like there is no safe zone. Maybe you've lost something really important to you. Or you've had to move to a new school. Or your parents have split up. Or someone you love died. In the middle of "storms" like that, you can't see any way out. So the only option left is to panic! Right?

Maybe not. Check out what Jesus did in the middle of a very real storm:

When evening came, Jesus said to his disciples, "Let's go over to the other side of the lake." They left the crowd behind. And they took him along in a boat, just as he was. There were also other boats with him.

A wild storm came up. Waves crashed over the boat. It was about to sink. Jesus was in the back, sleeping on a cushion. The disciples woke him up. They said, "Teacher! Don't you care if we drown?"

He got up and ordered the wind to stop. He said to the waves, "Quiet! Be still!" Then the wind died down. And it was completely calm.

He said to his disciples, "Why are you so afraid? Don't you have any faith at all yet?"

They were terrified. They asked each other, "Who is this? Even the wind and the waves obey him!"

Mark 4:35-41, NIrV

Think about it: Jesus was in the middle of a terrible storm. Wind was howling. Waves were crashing over the boat. He and His closest friends were in real danger of drowning. But Jesus was completely calm (calm enough to fall asleep!). And when His friends came to Him in a total panic, He simply told the storm to stop. "Quiet! Be still!" As if the storm were a pesky little brother.

Why do you think Jesus could be so calm—so unbothered—by a life-threatening storm?

Jesus was in control. He wasn't focused on the storm. He was focused on His Father, God. He showed the disciples that no matter what happens, God is always there. And God is always in control.

What storms are going on in your life? Not the thunder and lightning kind of storms. What "storms" keep you up worrying at night? What "storms" make your stomach feel tight and your heart race when you think about them too much?

Write your answers inside the storm cloud on the next page.

Take a minute to pray and ask for God's peace. You can say something like: "God, I am afraid of this storm. It's bigger than me. But it's not bigger than You. Can You remind me how big You are? Can You help me trust that You are bigger than this storm? Please give me Your peace." ★

DAY 3

HOW CAN PEACE POWER UP MY LIFE?
John 14:27

Draw a line from one piece of a broken object to its other half.

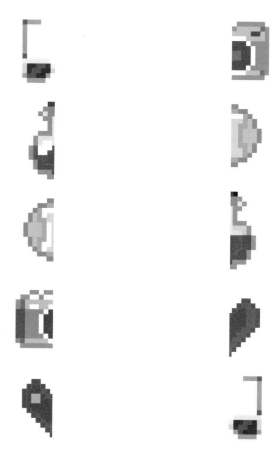

Have you ever broken something really valuable? What was it? What happened?

_____

_____

_____

_____

_____

If you were lucky, you broke something like a plate and it broke cleanly in half and it was easily fixed with a little super glue. If you weren't so lucky, it was something like a computer and no amount of super glue could help (especially if super glue ruined it in the first place).

Things break all the time. We fix them or replace them, but no matter what, they aren't exactly like they were before the big break. We can always see that tiny super glue-filled crack.

But when Jesus came, He came to fix more than a plate or some expensive electronics. He came to fix the _whole world_. The world was broken by sin. God was on one side of the crack and we were on the other. And Jesus fixed it _perfectly_. Jesus put us back together with God. No tiny crack. No annoying software update.

Let me explain. When human beings sinned, it broke their relationship with God. They became separated from Him—a perfect God couldn't be close to a bunch of really imperfect people. But when Jesus died to take the punishment for our sin and then came back to life, He put God and people back together again. Jesus made it possible for people to have a relationship with God that would last forever. When we ask Jesus to forgive us and be our Savior, He will. No matter how badly we sin. When we put our trust in Jesus and what He did for us, we'll get to live with Him forever in heaven.

This is why we say that Jesus came to bring us peace. The kind of peace that only Jesus has the power to give. Jesus said:

"I leave my peace with you. I give my peace to you. I do not give it to you as the world does. Do not let your hearts be troubled. And do not be afraid."

John 14:27, NIrV

SUPERNATURAL means beyond what is natural or normal.

When Jesus left this world, He gave us—anyone who believes in Him—His perfect, world-healing, super-powerful, **supernatural** peace.

He makes it possible for us to live unafraid. To not be troubled or worried all the time. Those feelings are going to creep in sometimes. But when we love Jesus and follow what He taught, we have the power—HIS power—to fight those scary feelings. ★

LOOK OUT!
A hazard to peace is worrying.

Have you ever drifted off the path into super-sticky mud or water when playing Mario Kart? The faster you get out, the better. But if you just follow the mud deeper and deeper, it's going to take a while to get back to a clear and quick path. Worrying is kind of like that sticky Mario Kart muck. It's almost impossible to avoid. But once you catch yourself worrying, the quicker you turn your thoughts to Jesus and ask Him to help you trust Him, the faster you'll get back to His peace. The longer you spend wallowing in worry, the harder it will be to find your way back to living in God's peace.

DAY 4

HOW DID PEOPLE IN THE BIBLE SHOW PEACE?
Luke 22:39-44

Would you go to a daycare to discuss Minecraft tips?

Would you go to a swim coach for piano lessons?

Would you go to a math teacher to learn how to be a master chef?

How about a cowboy for advice on the fashion industry?

Of course not. (Except maybe for that last one. Cowboys do know how to rock some bold fashion choices.) The point is, when you want to learn something new, you go to an expert. Someone who has been there, done that.

It's no different when learning how to "grow" the fruit of the Spirit. (Remember, the Holy Spirit's fruit produces awesome things in us, like love, joy, and peace.) When you're learning how to have peace—God's peace—who better to go to for help than the One called the Prince of Peace? Jesus Himself?

You may be thinking, "Yeah, right. When did Jesus ever have a math test over impossible fractions?" Or, "Jesus didn't have to put up with my annoying little brother." Or, "Jesus never had to leave all His friends and move somewhere new."

Well, you'd be surprised. While Jesus was on earth, He had troubles like you do. He may not have had the exact same worries and fears, but you would probably be surprised how similar His problems were to yours. In fact, He had even bigger worries and fears than you will ever have.

Check out what Luke wrote, just before Jesus was arrested and killed:

Jesus went out as usual to the Mount of Olives. His disciples followed him. When they reached the place, Jesus spoke. "Pray that you won't fall into sin when you are tempted," he said to them.

Then he went a short distance away from them. There he got down on his knees and prayed. He said, "Father, if you are willing, take this cup of suffering away from me. But do what you want, not what I want."

This means Jesus knew He was going to die to take the punishment for our sin.

An angel from heaven appeared to Jesus and gave him strength. Because he was very sad and troubled, he prayed even harder. His sweat was like drops of blood falling to the ground.

Luke 22:39-44, NIrV

Can you imagine how worried you would be if you knew at any moment you would be arrested and killed? So worried your sweat was like actual blood?

Even though Jesus is God's Son, He was also human. He knows how we feel. That means Jesus knows what it's like to be a kid. He knows what it's like to go to school and to grow up with siblings and to sometimes feel like you don't have friends. He felt the things you feel: happiness, anger, love, loneliness, excitement, sadness. He also knows what pain feels like.

Being human is hard. The truth is, you aren't in control of the things that happen to you. You're only in control of your own actions. And the only way to be okay with that—to have peace—is to turn to the One who is in control of everything. Just like Jesus did.

What is one thing you find yourself worrying about more than praying about?

_____

_____

_____

_____

_____

Talk to God and tell Him about it right now. ★

DAY 5

POWER UP
1 Peter 5:7 and Galatians 6:2

Put a check mark next to your favorite games to play with others. (Use the blanks to fill in any I missed!)

☐ Chess

☐ Roblox

☐ Tag

☐ Hide and seek

☐ Mario Kart

☐ Battleship

☐ Fortnite

☐ Twister

☐ Just Dance

☐ Risk

☐ Sequence

☐ Pokémon Go

☐ Monopoly

☐ Bananagram

☐ Settlers of Catan

☐ Ticket to Ride

☐ Clue

☐ _____

☐ _____

☐ _____

Why do you like having other people to play these games with?

Are there games that are easier when you play them in a group?

Whether it's Pokémon Go, Roblox, or taking turns on Pac-Man, games are more fun with friends around. And, depending on the game, other people can even help you defeat an enemy faster, collect more materials, share powers, or help look out for hazards.

The same is true in life.

Pro Tip #10:

When you play Minecraft with another pro, you might just learn a new pro tip or 20. (I think that pro tip can count for at least 10 tips).

Sometimes life can get a little too crazy to deal with alone. So many things are going on at once. There's so much you feel like you have to worry about that your stress level goes through the roof. At those times, it can feel like having peace is impossible.

The good news is, you don't have to deal with it all alone. You can look in the Bible to know what to do when things get overwhelming, when anxiety is out of control, and peace is out of reach:

Turn all your worries over to him. He cares about you.

1 Peter 5:7, NIrV

Carry one another's heavy loads. If you do, you will fulfill the law of Christ.

Galatians 6:2, NIrV

When life feels too heavy—when big and scary things are happening—talk about those things with God and with other people. God wants you to ask for help. He wants you to turn to Him when you feel anxious. He wants you to ask someone you trust to help you when you feel **overwhelmed**.

OVERWHELMED means dazed or defeated.

The truth is, games are more fun when we play them with others. Just like life is better when we live it with others.

Write the names of five people you can go to when you feel overwhelmed. Who can you talk to when your worries get too big? (The first one's filled in for you.) One or two can be friends your age, but make sure you have a few adults in there, too. Adults usually have a lot more practice dealing with big worries.

LIST OF PEOPLE TO HELP CARRY MY LOAD:

1 *God*

2

3

4

5

Now that you have your list of people, let them know! **Grab five pieces of paper or small notes and write this down on each note (filling in the names):**

Hey, _____ !

Sometimes I don't know what to do with all my worries. In Galatians 6:2, Paul tells us to carry one another's heavy loads. If it's okay with you, I'd like to talk to you whenever I feel anxious. Thanks for being there for me and helping me carry my worries when they get too heavy.

Sincerely,

_____

POWER UP CHALLENGE

Week three is a wrap, and you are powering up like a Ninja Turtle with a belly full of pizza.

First things first: Did your devotional partner memorize Philippians 4:6?

☐ YES   ☐ NO

X _____

(sign your name here)

Bonus: What did you give your partner for memorizing the verse?

_____

Here's your personal Power Up Challenge. **Choose a warm and sunny day this week to spend a few minutes sitting outside.** It could be in your backyard or a nearby park (you may need to take an adult!). When you get to a cozy spot, set a timer (or ask the adult with you to set a timer), and sit for three minutes in silence. (Last time you sat for two minutes. I bet you can beat that this time!) You can take deep breaths, look around for small animals, close your eyes and listen, or simply talk to God.

When the three minutes are up, answer these questions. Write your answers here or simply think about the questions in your head. ★

What did you think about?

How do you feel after your three minutes of peace?

Do you think the rest of your day will be any different because of it?

Was it helpful? How?

Will you make time to do that again? When?

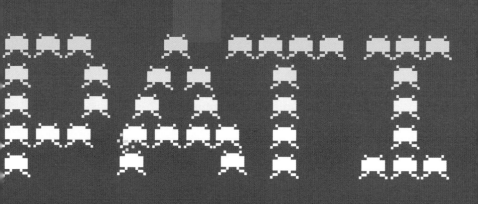

LEVEL FOUR

WEEK 4

PATIENCE

Patience is (arguably) the most difficult part of the fruit of the Spirit to master. Don't believe me? Close your eyes and imagine the look on your mom's face when you tell her you left your jacket at school . . . again. Or when she tells you to "PUT. YOUR. SHOES. ON!" for, like, the tenth time in a row.

Yikes. Not exactly a perfect picture of patience.

The truth is, when we think about patience, we think about waiting until later for what we want now. Which is hard. But it's more than that. Patience is also about how you act and feel while you're waiting. Anyone can wait. But it takes a **super**-patient person not to whine or go into fits of rage while waiting.

SUPER means very, extremely, or more than.

In your own words, what does it mean to be patient?

_____

_____

_____

_____

_____

Great! Before you turn the page, remind your partner of this week's Memory Verse Challenge. ★

> Everyone should be quick to listen.
> But they should be slow to speak.
> They should be slow to get angry.
>
> **James 1:19b, NIrV**

Pro Tip #11:

To make all your Pokémon evolve (or grow), keep playing and have a little patience.

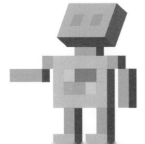

DAY 1

WHAT IS PATIENCE?
James 1:19b

What is your favorite day of the year? (Check the word search for some possibilities.) Maybe it's Christmas. Or your birthday—the only day of the year that's all about YOU. Unless you're a twin . . . or your birthday is on Christmas. Maybe your favorite day of the year is Thanksgiving, or maybe it's a whole week in April when your favorite game store has buy-one-get-one free video games.

Favorite Day Word Search

```
F B B Z N S V Y R V E W L S T
W I Y T T E A F A K A I N R H
S O E Z G D E L N L S V O A A
I D Q L H X E W G R T F S E N
Q J Y T D N O J O W E R Q Y K
F D R V T D T Q B L R P Z W S
S I V I P G A G E S L S M E G
B A N F N J K Y Y X Z A S N I
R E S A M T S I R H C U H Z V
S H S A T U R D A Y N K V O I
A J Y X U U Y K W D U J X F N
N Z A J T K P K A O O Q Y I G
H M J H C N G Y Z F T B I A X
D S N T U H G N Z S I Q U Y T
X M P B R R A A G U F V V X N
```

WORD BOX

Christmas
New Year
Birthday
Valentine's
Easter
Halloween
Saturday
Sunday
Thanksgiving
Field day

So, what is your favorite day? _____

Why? _____

_____

Great! (That's my favorite day, too). And let me guess. You wake up every other day of the year angry. Angry that it's not your favorite day. Angry that there are still a whole bunch of days before it's your favorite day again. Angry that you don't get to do any of your favorite day things. You stomp everywhere you go. You huff and puff and refuse to smile. You don't eat or talk to anyone. You are angry every other day of the year. Angry, angry, angry.

No? Oh, good. That would be a pretty miserable life for you.

It can be hard to wait for something really exciting like your birthday. But if you throw a fit every day because it's not your birthday, you'd miss out on . . .

game nights,
sleepovers with friends,
big family meals with Grandma,
playing with all your neighborhood friends,
or just quiet afternoons reading a book.

The same is true about waiting for smaller things—from waiting in line at a restaurant to some fun weekend plans. Check this out:

> Everyone should be quick to listen. But they should be slow to speak. They should be slow to get angry.
>
> **James 1:19b, NIrV**

Let's face it. When you realize you have to wait for dessert, or you have to save up for that video game, or today is not your birthday, your first response might be anger. But anger doesn't change anything. It doesn't make time go faster. You still have to wait.

James (Jesus' own brother) tells us to be slow to speak and slow to get angry. In other words, when you hear something you don't like, something that makes you angry, or something that makes you feel super-impatient, pause. Take a deep breath. Ask yourself, "How do I want to spend my time waiting?" And then maybe have some fun between now and then—you know, instead of slamming your door 182 times.

What things are you waiting on now?

_____

_____

_____

_____

What good things might happen between now and then?

_____

_____

_____

_____ ★

Pro Tip #12:

There may not be shortcuts in life, but there
sure are some great ones in Mario Kart.

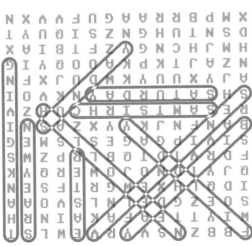

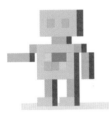

Favorite Day Word Search Answers:

DAY 2

HOW DOES GOD SHOW PATIENCE?
Psalm 103:8

Picture this: It's summertime. All the aunts and uncles and cousins are getting together to watch fireworks at your grandpa's house. You're carrying your mom's famous American flag berry cake to the car when you step on that shoelace she told you to tie. Before you know it, you're on the ground surrounded by smashed cake bits and a cracked cake pan.

Or how about this? You flop onto the couch first thing Saturday morning. You turn on your favorite TV show. You swing your feet up on the coffee table to get comfy and accidentally kick over your dad's fresh cup of coffee . . . spilling it all over his open laptop.

What character (from a video game, TV show, movie, or book) would your parent turn into in those moments? Draw it here.

If you answered something like a zombie pigman or the Hulk, that's because your parents are human. (Like many humans, they might have some work to do on this whole patience thing.)

But check out what King David wrote about God, your **superhuman** Father:

Remember what SUPER means? It means "more than." So SUPERHUMAN means going beyond human power.

> The Lord is tender and kind. He is gracious. He is slow to get angry. He is full of love.
>
> **Psalm 103:8, NIrV**

When you sin, God is gracious. He is slow to get angry. He is full of love. He doesn't turn into a zombie pigman. Anger doesn't just explode from Him. God is patient with you.

Think about this. God knows everything that's going to happen before it happens. So He knows what everyone is going to do before they do it. That means that God knew that:

Adam and Eve were going to disobey Him.

Cain was going to kill his brother Abel.

The Israelites were going to worship a golden cow they had made.

Samson was going to break his vow.

Jonah was going to hide from God in a boat.

God knew all of that. He knew it was going to happen long before it did. But when it did, God stuck by His people. Day in and day out. He was working, patiently, to save His people even though they were breaking His heart around nearly every turn. God is patient and slow to anger.

The Bible is full of examples of people who did wrong. But God still sent His much-loved only Son to die to save them.

And this goes for you too. God has patiently loved you for a long time. Jesus died for your sins—before you were even alive to commit the first one.

So if you're having trouble being patient, why not go to the One who has shown the most patience ever? Over thousands and thousands of years? Take a minute and think of a time you have the most trouble showing patience. Ask God for some ideas—some ways you could get better at showing patience. Then, be patient!

Answers might not come right away, but when they do, write them down on the next page.

I can show patience by _____

_____

_____

_____

_____

_____

_____

_____ ★

DAY 3

HOW CAN PATIENCE POWER UP MY LIFE?
Isaiah 40:31

Kids all over the world spent the summer of 2016 meeting up with friends, getting outside, exploring their neighborhoods, and playing a new game: Pokémon Go. Within a few hours of its release, over a million people had downloaded the app. Over the following months, that number grew by hundreds of millions. Now the app has over a billion downloads and more than $2 billion spent in in-app purchases.

Pro Tip #13:
Don't spend $1 billion on Pokémon Go in-app purchases.

If you've ever played Pokémon Go or another Pokémon game, you know the quickest way to win battles is by evolving (growing) your Pokémon. Charmander may start off as an adorable little squishy guy. But after a while, Charmander gets a little stronger and becomes Charmeleon. Then before you know it, your cute little squishy Pokémon is a super-strong, flying Charizard!

Just for fun, if you could evolve like a Pokémon, what would your new names be? And what new powers would you have?

NAME	POWER

In a way, we are all little Pokémon—starting off super-cute and growing into bigger, stronger, smarter people. But instead of fire or flying powers, we can have fruit-of-the-Spirit kind of powers. As we grow up and mature, we learn how things like patience actually make us stronger, better versions of ourselves. But in order to have (and show) patience, you have to be super-strong. You have to be strong enough to fight off the urge to shout all the reasons it's not fair. You have to be strong enough not to whine. Strong enough to focus on something else. And that can take **supernatural** strength. Isaiah (eye-ZAY-uh) tells us in the Bible:

Remember what SUPERNATURAL means?

But those who trust in the Lord will receive new strength. They will fly as high as eagles. They will run and not get tired. They will walk and not grow weak.

Isaiah 40:31, NIrV

Showing patience can be exhausting, especially when you try to do it all by yourself. But when you trust God, when you pray and ask for His help, you can have the kind of patience that doesn't get tired or weak. You can have the strength to keep waiting—with a good attitude. ★

LOOK OUT!
A hazard to patience is complaining.

Little Charmander will never evolve into Charizard if you only focus on collecting more and more Pokémon. In order for your little monsters to grow, you have to focus on what you *do* have instead of what you *don't* have. The same is true about patience. When you are focused on the things that are going wrong or the things you don't have, you can't show patience. You can't power up with the Holy Spirit when you are stuck looking for more and more things to complain about.

DAY 4

HOW DID PEOPLE IN THE BIBLE SHOW PATIENCE?
Luke 2:25-28

Can you fill in the day of the year the following holidays are on?

We'll start with a couple of easy ones:

Your birthday	
New Year's Day	
The Fourth of July	

Great! Now some that might be a little harder:

Valentine's Day	
Christmas Day	
Mother's Day	

Do you know any of these?

Earth Day	
Veterans Day	
St. Patrick's Day	

You may not know the dates of all those holidays, but you probably know which month or at least which season they are in. Especially the one where you get out of school and get a bunch of presents. That's right, Christmas. You probably know Christmas Day is December 25. You may even have one of those paper countdown chains counting the days until the next Christmas—starting every December 26.

But can you imagine not knowing when Christmas is coming? Like, not even knowing if there will *be* a Christmas this year? What if your parents said, "I promise we will celebrate Christmas again in your life, but I'm not saying when. It could be next week, next month, or in 20 years."

You might go crazy! It would be all you could think about! You would wake up every morning of your life asking the same question: "Is Christmas today?"

Which do you think would be harder? Circle one:

Being patient when
you know how long
you have to wait

Being patient when
you have no idea
how long you will
have to wait

There was a man in the Bible who had to wait. His name was Simeon (SIM-ee-un):

A GODLY person loves and respects God.

MESSIAH is another name for Jesus.

In Jerusalem there was a man named Simeon. He was a good and godly man. He was waiting for God's promise to Israel to come true. The Holy Spirit was with him. The Spirit had told Simeon that he would not die before he had seen the Lord's Messiah. The Spirit led him into the temple courtyard. Then Jesus' parents brought the child in. They came to do for him what the Law required. Simeon took Jesus in his arms and praised God.

Luke 2:25-28, NIrV

Simeon knew he would meet the Messiah. God had promised him that. But he didn't know when. He could have waited years, even decades, wondering if that day was the day. But Simeon was a "good and godly man," which means he probably showed a lot of patience, no matter how long he had to wait. And he got a pretty huge reward for his strength and patience: he got to hold God's Son as a baby.

Have you ever had to wait for something but you didn't know
when it was coming? Were you able to be patient? How?

_____

_____

_____

_____

_____

_____

_____ ★

DAY 5

POWER UP
Philippians 2:14

Just for fun, draw your favorite emoji here:

Now, draw an emoji of how you feel when an adult says
the following:

> "You can't go to your friend's house
> until your room is clean."

> "No sweets until after dinner!"

> "Have you studied for your test yet?"

Did you draw a peaceful-looking smiley face each time? No? How about side-eyes, eye rolls, or angry steam-eared faces? Probably more like it.

No one likes to be told they have to wait for something. We all want to do the fun stuff now. Eat all the cake now. Work and study never. But life doesn't work that way. No one gets to only do what they want, when they want. Not even adults. So why aren't we all walking around looking like THIS all day every day?

Patience.

If we complained or got angry every time we didn't get our way or had to wait, humans would be the worst. Seriously, you wouldn't want to be around anyone who did that. Sure, sometimes those emojis slip out. But check out what Paul wrote in the book of Philippians:

> **Do everything without complaining or arguing.**
>
> **Philippians 2:14, NIrV**

Whoa. *Everything?* How do you help with yardwork or clean out the cat's litter box without complaining?! It sounds impossible, but that's the kind of patience God's Holy Spirit gives us. That's the kind of patience that can power you up from . . .

 to

But how? There are a lot of things you can do each day to help you have more patience, to help you complain less (or not at all). Things like sleeping and eating enough, hanging out with positive people, and staying connected to God—the source of patience.

Over the next few days, pay close attention to your complaining. Write down what you find yourself complaining about the most.

Ask yourself a few questions:

Have I had enough sleep? YES or NO

Have I been hanging around positive, patient people? YES or NO

Have I been spending enough time with God ? YES or NO

If any of those answers is "No," try fixing it and see if you are able to have more patience.

A couple of ways to spend time with God are praying and reading the Bible.

POWER UP CHALLENGE

Time for your favorite part of the week: The Power Up Challenge that will take your patience to new levels. But WAIT! (See what I did there? Patience . . . wait . . . waiting?)

First things first: Did your adult devotional partner memorize James 1:19?

☐ YES   ☐ NO

X _____

(sign your name here)

Bonus: What did you give your partner for memorizing the verse?

_____

And now for your 4th Power Up Challenge:

See if you can go an entire day without complaining. From start to finish. Lights on to lights out. You might find it to be harder than it sounds. To set yourself up for success, make sure all these boxes are checked:

☐ Enough sleep
☐ Enough healthful food
☐ Positive people
☐ Connect with God
☐ Healthy outlets (see the next page)

We talked about the first four boxes yesterday. We need to eat and sleep well, surround ourselves with positive, patient people, and stay connected to the source of patience: God. But the fifth one—healthy outlets—is new.

When you can't do or have what you want right now, and anger starts to build up in your chest, what can you do to release that anger in a healthy way? (Hint: Complaining is not healthy.)

Here are a few healthy options:

- Stand on your head as long as you can
- Take three slow, deep breaths
- Run around outside (tell an adult first)
- Ride your bike
- Listen to your favorite music
- Stomp your feet (on bubble wrap if you have it!)
- Jump as far as you can
- Rip up (parent-approved) newspaper
- Play (nicely) with a pet

Now that you have all the tools, see if you can make it through a whole day without complaining. At the end of the day, come back here and write down how it went:

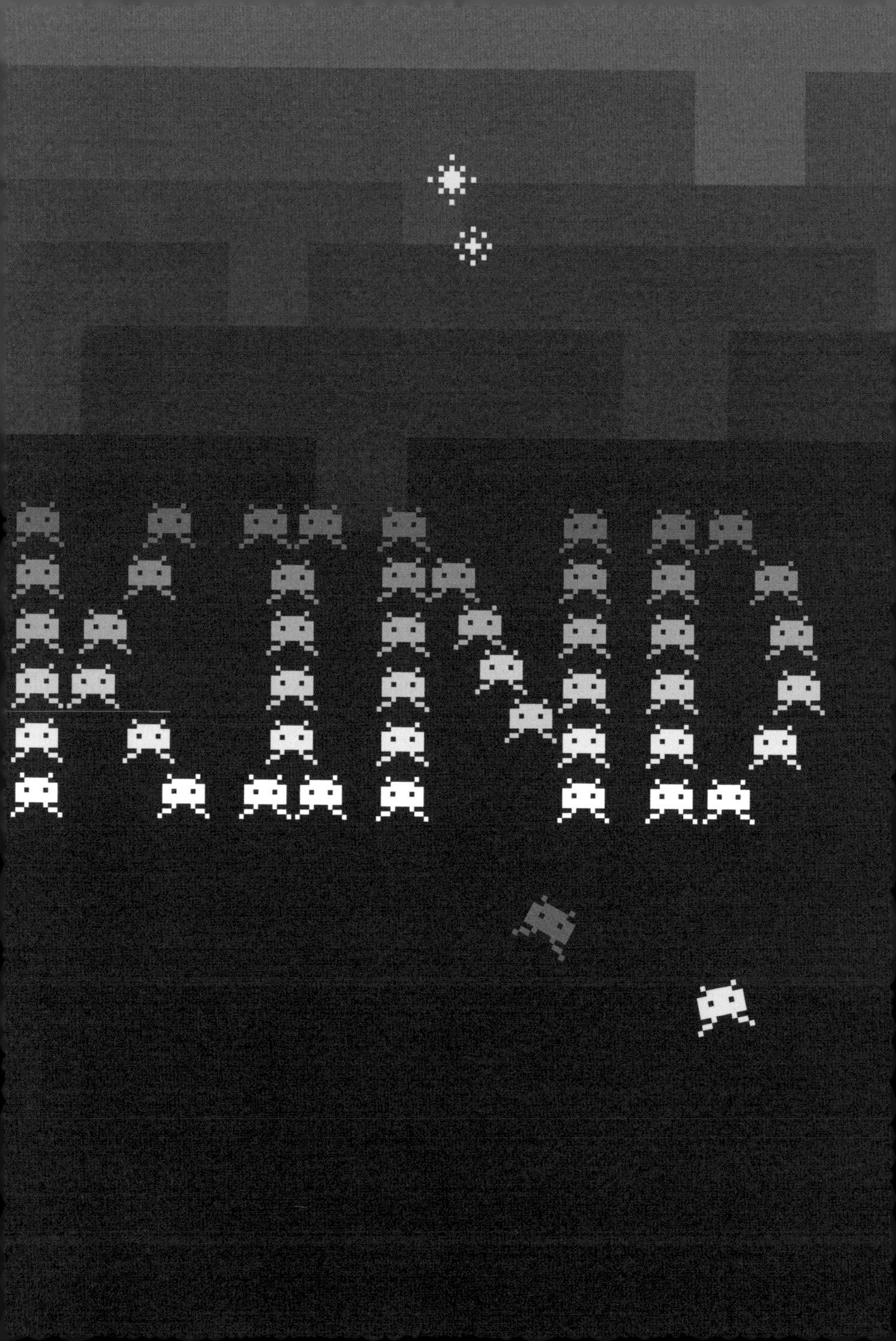
KIND

LEVEL FIVE

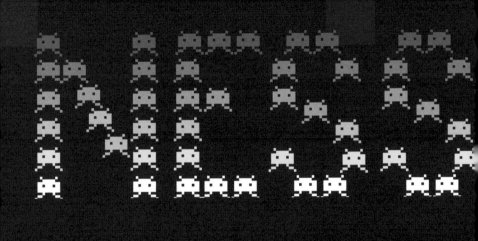

WEEK 5

KINDNESS

"Be kind." You've probably heard those words dozens of times (maybe a dozen times already today). But what does it look like to be kind?

Define "kindness" in your own words:

_____

_____

_____

_____

This week, we are going to find out how God defines kindness. And you might be surprised by how BIG His idea of kindness really is. But before you turn the page, here's your new **Memory Verse Challenge**. Don't forget to challenge your partner to memorize it; everyone needs more kindness in their life! ★

You are God's chosen people. You are holy and dearly loved. So put on tender mercy and kindness as if they were your clothes. Don't be proud. Be gentle and patient.

Colossians 3:12, NIrV

DAY 1

WHAT IS KINDNESS?
Colossians 3:12

What do you put on in the mornings?
Check all that apply:

- ☐ shirt
- ☐ pants
- ☐ underwear
- ☐ socks
- ☐ shoes
- ☐ kindness
- ☐ deodorant
- ☐ belt
- ☐ hair gel
- ☐ hat
- ☐ sunglasses

Pro Tip #14:

Diamond armor is a pretty great thing to put on in Minecraft.

Wait—kindness? Did that just say *kindness*?
Putting on socks and shoes . . . that makes sense.
But putting on kindness? How do you do that?

You may not understand everything about kindness, but you're
pretty sure it's not something you keep in your closet. And
you're right. It's not a thing you can see, hold, or touch. But read
this verse again that Paul wrote in the book of Colossians:

You are God's chosen people. You are holy and dearly
loved. So put on tender mercy and kindness as if they were
your clothes. Don't be proud. Be gentle and patient.

Colossians 3:12, NIrV

God wants kindness to be a habit. He wants it to be so easy you don't even think about it—like putting on your clothes in the morning. But what is kindness? Once you put it on, then what?

Kindness is showing others they are valuable by how you treat them.

In other words, being kind means you know every person's . . .

- **opinions**
- **thoughts**
- **feelings**
- **needs**
- **likes**
- **dislikes**

. . . matter because every person is valuable. Check out the way the Colossians verse breaks it down:

> **Don't be proud.** Include everyone in your game. Don't think you are too good, too cool, too smart, too anything to include someone. Know that everyone is just as important as you are. And let your actions show you believe that.
>
> **Be gentle.** When someone is hurting, be the one who offers comfort. Say encouraging words. Let others go before you. Think of others' needs first.
>
> **Be patient.** Remember this one from last week? When someone hurts or frustrates you, be slow to anger. Be quick to forgive.

Those things sound simple but they can be super-hard sometimes. We don't always *feel* kind. Sometimes we feel the *opposite* of kind. But if you practice kindness *every day*—if you put it on each morning like your favorite worn-out hat—it starts to become a habit.

Find something you wear a lot. It could be a hat, necklace, belt, or pair of shoes. With an adult's permission, choose a way to write "Colossians 3:12" on it somewhere you (and maybe only you) will see when you put it on. Maybe you write the verse under the brim of your hat, on the inside of your belt, or on the bottom of your sneakers.

Then, each time you put on that item of clothing, remind yourself that you are putting on kindness. You are putting on humility (not being proud), gentleness, and patience. Then go about your day, showing others how valuable they are by how you treat them. ★

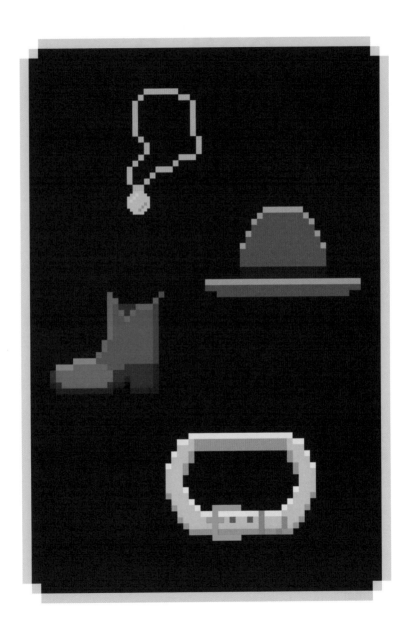

DAY 2

HOW DOES GOD SHOW KINDNESS?
Titus 3:4-6

Do you know about how much these items cost? **Take a guess.**

Xbox One _____

Nintendo Switch _____

Super Smash Bros. game _____

Pokémon: Let's Go game _____

PlayStation 4 controller _____

Maybe you know nothing about video games. So you have no idea what they cost. Maybe you know exactly what they cost because you've been saving up to buy one for nearly a year. Either way, you know they aren't cheap. And *definitely* not free.

But what if they *were* free?

Stay with me for a minute. What if you went to your favorite game store and the owner of the store said,

"Hey, _____ *your name* _____ ! I'm so glad you're here. And just to show how glad I am, why don't you take that Xbox . . . for free!"

That may sound crazy, but it's exactly what God did for you. Well, not exactly. I mean, God never owned a video game store. You'll see what I mean when you read these verses from the book of Titus. **Fill in the blanks with words from the word box.**

"But the _____ and love of God

our Savior appeared. He _____ us.

It wasn't because of the good things we had done. It was

because of his mercy. He saved us by washing away our

_____. We were born again. The Holy

Spirit gave us _____ life. God poured out

the Spirit on us _____ because of what

_____ Christ our Savior has done."

Titus 3:4-6 NIrV

WORD BOX

Choose words from below to fill in the blanks above. Check your work in the Bible or a Bible app.

patience	mistakes
kindness	sins
loved	new
Jesus	freely
old	responsibly
hated	saved

Did you see that word "freely"? God loves us so much, He sent Jesus to take the punishment for our sin. For *free*. You can't earn closeness with God. There's no way to pay for eternal life with God in heaven . . . because Jesus already paid for it. He did that for us out of kindness and love.

But that's not all. When we ask Jesus to save us, His Holy Spirit comes to live inside of us and will always be with us. He gives us the Holy Spirit so that we will have . . .

★ love   ★ joy   ★ peace

★ patience   ★ kindness   ★ goodness

★ faithfulness   ★ gentleness   ★ self-control

The Holy Spirit grows fruit in us (like kindness) to make life better and a little easier. It's like He gives us new life here on earth with these power ups. And He did all of that for you. For free. Because He thinks you are really, really, super-duper valuable. And He wanted to show you how valuable you really are.

How kind is God?
(On a scale from Ultimate Kindness to Mic Drop Kindness)

Ultimate Kindness

Mic Drop Kindness

●||||||||||||||||||||||||||||||||||||||||||||||||||||||||||||||||||||||||||||●

(Did you have a hard time deciding how to mark the scale? If you did, then you got the point! It's hard to give God a "grade" for kindness, because His kindness is so immense it's hard to measure.)

Take a minute to thank God for His kindness. Thank Him for giving it freely. And ask Him to help you see others the way He sees them, as really, really, super-duper valuable. ★

DAY 3

HOW CAN KINDNESS POWER UP MY LIFE?
Romans 12:20-21

Brrrrrrrrriiiiiiiinng! Your alarm clock jolts you out of a deep sleep. You climb out of bed, walk down the hall, and see the bathroom door already closed and locked. Your sister got there first. You bang on the door. All you need is your toothbrush and toothpaste, but she just yells, "You snooze, you lose!" and laughs.

By the time she's done, you only have Five minutes to brush your teeth and grab whatever breakfast you can. You hear the bus coming down the hill as you open the pantry to find an empty box of Pop Tarts. You see your sister, Pop Tart in hand, skipping out the door. There's no time to make anything else, so you slam the door and run.

Your stomach growls all the way to school and through your first class. But suddenly a plan hits you. You ask to go to the bathroom. On your way, you pass your sister's classroom. Her lunchbox is hanging on a hook outside the door. You make sure no one's looking. You grab the lunchbox and dump the contents in the bathroom trash (not before wolfing down the baggie of Oreos she packed).

Your sister is SO mad after school that she runs inside the house, grabs your journal, and sends photos of it to all her friends. You pour an entire bottle of shampoo in her backpack. She writes on your face in permanent marker while you're sleeping. You fill her toothpaste tube with hot sauce. She replaces the cream in your Oreos with her spicy toothpaste.

A whole week goes by and it feels like the cycle will never stop. You are so mad you can't think about anything else. You can't eat or sleep, in fear of what your sister will do next. Instead of homework, chores, or playing with friends, you spend all your time planning your next revenge. What will be the ultimate, final move to put an end to it all? But of course, your sister figures it out first.

One morning, she pokes her head in your room and says, "Want to use the bathroom first?" You're almost too scared to say yes, but it's picture day and you really need the few extra minutes.

You cautiously open the bathroom door . . . and find a long apology written on the bathroom mirror. You read how sorry your sister is and how much she misses just talking and being your friend. Your shoulders relax (you didn't know how stressed you were). All the anger disappears. You smile (for, like, the first time in a week). And everything is okay (for now).

Have you ever gotten in a revenge battle like that? (Okay, maybe not quite that epic.) Fighting can feel like a full-time job. One that just ends up making you angrier and angrier. Believe it or not, Paul tells us the ultimate revenge move in the book of Romans:

Scripture says, "If your enemies are hungry, give them food to eat. If they are thirsty, give them something to drink. By doing those things, you will pile up burning coals on their heads." Don't let evil overcome you. Overcome evil by doing good.

Romans 12:20-21, NIrV

This means to repay meanness with kindness, which can make someone feel bad for being mean. It could help them change their behavior.

"Burning coals" on your enemy's head?! Brutal.

But there's a point.

Take the story on the last couple of pages, for example. There are a few points in the story where choosing kindness could have put an end to the sisters' all-out war. The girls' revenge tactics were epic, but in the end, they just caused more pain (and hunger).

Take a pen or pencil and rewrite the story using the space in the margins. Choose one spot where kindness could have made everything better. Draw a line through the unkind action and write what would happen in your kinder version.

Kindness is super-powerful. It can overcome evil. It can put an end to the fighting. And it might just put an end to an enemy . . . by making them a friend. ★

LOOK OUT!
A hazard to kindess is
excluding others.

When you leave people out on purpose, you make them feel unimportant. You show them they aren't valuable at all. And you might miss out on a really great friendship.

DAY 4

HOW DID PEOPLE IN THE BIBLE SHOW KINDNESS?
Luke 10:25-37

Before . . .

Mario and Bowser
Link and Ganondorf
Luke Skywalker and Darth Vader
Dumbledore and Grindelwald
Gandalf and Sauron

. . . there were the Jews and the Samaritans. Okay, maybe that's a little dramatic. But the Jews and the Samaritans really, really, really, really did not get along. Maybe it was because the Jews destroyed the Samaritans' **temple**. Maybe it was because the Samaritans scattered bones in the Jewish temple . . . on Passover. (True stories.)

A TEMPLE is a place of worship.

However it started, the Jews thought the Samaritans were evil and the Samaritans thought the same about the Jews—which is what made this story that Jesus told super-wild:

"A [Jewish] man was going down from Jerusalem to Jericho. Robbers attacked him. They stripped off his clothes and beat him. Then they went away, leaving him almost dead. A priest happened to be going down that same road. When he saw the man, he passed by on the other side. A Levite also came by. When he saw the man, he passed by on the other side too.

> **A PRIEST is someone who speaks to God for others.**

> **A LEVITE is a type of priest.**

"But a Samaritan came to the place where the man was. When he saw the man, he felt sorry for him. He went to him, poured olive oil and wine on his wounds and bandaged them. Then he put the man on his own donkey. He took him to an inn and took care of him. The next day he took out two silver coins. He gave them to the owner of the inn. 'Take care of him,' he said. 'When I return, I will pay you back for any extra expense you may have.'"

Luke 10:30-35, NIrV

Thanks to this story, most people think of the word "good" when they hear "Samaritan" these days. But the day Jesus told this story, "good" was the last word those listening would have used to describe a Samaritan. Bad. Evil. Wrong. Gross. Bone-scattering-crazy-person, sure. But not "good." Never "good."

That's exactly why Jesus used a Samaritan as the hero of the story. It's easy to be kind to the people you think are good. But the fruit-of-the-Spirit kind of kindness means showing everyone they are valuable, no matter what. Because the truth is, no one is all good or all bad.

Think about it: Even Darth Vader saves Luke Skywalker's life in the end.

Has there ever been a time when someone did something unexpected and kind for you? Maybe your brother gave you a compliment, and it sounded like he really meant it. Maybe your mom took you out for ice cream, even though she's usually Captain Sugar Police. Maybe that kid at church who's always grumpy showed real understanding when you shared your prayer request. **Think about it and write or draw about a time like that here:**

Then, show that person how much his or her kindness meant to you by saying thanks. You can write a note, send a text, or say thanks the next time you see them. You can even pray and thank God for putting that person in your life at just the right time. ★

DAY 5

POWER UP
James 2:1-4

Underline your choice in each of the following sentences.

Would you rather . . .

live in space or under the sea?

speak every language in the world or play every musical instrument?

be the funniest person alive or the smartest person alive?

eat donuts or candy?

design a new video game or direct a movie?

We all have preferences, things we would rather have or do if we had a choice. A lot of the time, those preferences help us decide who our friends are. If you really like musical instruments, you probably choose friends who also like music. If you are super into game coding, you probably have friends you can talk with about Python and JavaScript. Or maybe you love donuts so much you have formed a donut club at school and you all take turns bringing in a dozen donuts each Friday.

Getting along with some people more than others is just part of life. It's okay. But while you may not be friends with everyone, God wants you to be *kind* to everyone. Check out this scenario that James wrote about in his book of the Bible (called James).

My brothers and sisters, you are believers in our glorious Lord Jesus Christ. So treat everyone the same. Suppose a man comes into your meeting wearing a gold ring and fine clothes. And suppose a poor man in dirty old clothes also comes in. Would you show special attention to the one who is wearing fine clothes? Would you say, "Here's a good seat for you"? Would you say to the poor person, "You stand there"? Or "Sit on the floor by my feet"? If you would, aren't you treating some people better than others? Aren't you like judges who have evil thoughts?

James 2:1-4, NIrV

As **Christians**, we know that God made and loves every single person on this planet. We know each person is just as valuable as the next. And we know God loves us all equally. So, God wants us to treat all people with kindness. He wants us to treat everyone equally.

A CHRISTIAN is a follower of Jesus.

You can't invite everyone God loves to a sleepover at your house. You can't make chocolate chip cookies for every person in the world.

But you can . . .

> smile at everyone you see.
> notice—and try to help—when anyone is having a hard time.
> stand up for everyone.
> give compliments and encouragement to everyone.
> use manners (say thank you and please) with everyone.
> be a good listener to everyone.

Are there people you treat differently because of the way they look or act? **Read the following sentences. Fill in the blanks with the unscrambled words. Then put these ideas into action!** ★

_____ _____ _____ _____ _____ about how someone else is feeling.

T   k   h   n   i

_____ _____ _____ _____ a compliment.

G   v   e   i

_____ _____ _____ _____ _____ _____ a new friend to play.

v   l   t   n   i   e

_____ _____ _____ _____ a pencil to a friend.

e   d   n   L

___ ___ ___ ___ ___ someone who has helped you.

T   n   h   a   k

___ ___ ___ ___ ___ at 25 people.

m   l   i   e   S

___ ___ ___ ___ a card to a new friend.

S   n   e   d

___ ___ ___ ___ ___ at a local homeless shelter.

e   S   r   e   v

Answers to the Fill in the Blanks:

Thank someone who has helped you.

Smile at 25 people.

Send a card to a new friend.

Serve at a local homeless shelter.

Think about how someone else is feeling.

Give a compliment.

Invite a new friend to play.

Lend a pencil to a friend.

POWER UP CHALLENGE

You learned a lot about kindness this week—the kindness that comes straight from God. Are you ready to power up and put your kindness into action?

First things first: Did your devotional partner memorize Colossians 3:12?

☐ YES   ☐ NO

X _____

(sign your name here)

Bonus: What did you give your partner for memorizing the verse?

_____

Over the next few days, you (and anyone else you invite) will be playing Kindness Bingo. If you've never played the classic game Bingo, the goal is to check off one whole row of squares vertically, horizontally, or diagonally. Can you guess the way you check off squares in Kindness Bingo? You got it: by doing the act of kindness written on the square. So challenge yourself or your friends and see how quickly you can complete a row of kind acts.

As you play, think about how each act of kindness makes you feel. Side effects of Kindness Bingo may include: joy, sudden hugs, laughter, a warm or tingly feeling, and new friends. ★

Kindness Bingo

Put change in a vending machine	Donate to a food pantry	Let someone go ahead of you in line	Take candy to your teacher, coach, or small group leader
Make someone else's bed	Roll out your neighbor's garbage cans for them	Mail a handwritten note to a friend	Smile at 10 people
Leave a dish of fresh water out for neighborhood dogs	Play with someone new	Donate towels and blankets to an animal shelter	Leave $1 bills in the dollar store toy section
Open the door for someone whose hands are full	Compliment at least 5 people in one day	Tape bags of popcorn to movie rental machines	Set up a free lemonade stand

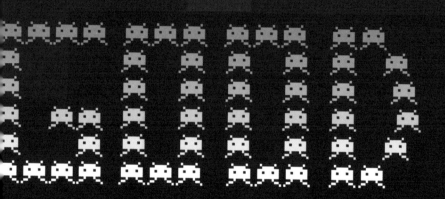

WEEK 6

GOODNESS

Think about the word "good." We use it to talk about lots of stuff. When the pizza is hot and tasty, we call it good. A movie that makes you laugh is good. Puppies, bowling, and a day spent at . . .

_____ your favorite place _____ are all good.

You know you want to be good *at* things, too, like slicing and dicing when playing Fruit Ninja. But what does it mean to be *good* in life?

Think about this: Something that is good is right. It's positive and helpful. It might be something we need. It might be something we like or enjoy. Something that is good is something that we want.

Here's a word you may not use as much: goodness.

Based on the definition of "good," explain "goodness" in your own words:

_____

_____

_____

_____

Check out what Jesus said about goodness. (Tip: This verse will be the Memory Verse Challenge for the week. Don't forget to share it with the adult you chose as a partner!)

> "A good person produces good things from the treasury of a good heart, and an evil person produces evil things from the treasury of an evil heart."
>
> **Matthew 12:35, NLT**

So, a good person does good things? And a not-so-good person does not-so-good things? (Sounds simple, right? We'll talk more about that later.)

Now, underline these words: "from the treasury of a good heart." That's important. But what does it mean? A treasury? In your heart? Are there, like, gold coins in a person's chest?

Buckle up, friends. Because this week, we're making like Mario Kart and going on a good, good ride to answer those questions, and more. ★

Pro Tip #15:

In Mario Kart, being in the lead isn't always a good thing. You'll receive weaker power ups. But if you're patient, and you save your power ups when you're not in the lead, they can come in handy later.

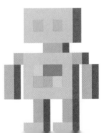

DAY 1

WHAT IS GOODNESS?
Matthew 12:35

Look at our **Memory Verse Challenge** again. **Fill in the words that are missing.** If you need help, flip back to page 147.

"A _____ person produces _____

things from the treasury of a _____ heart, and an

_____ person produces _____

things from the treasury of an _____ heart."

Matthew 12:35, NLT

Let's talk more about what that verse means. We said earlier that "good" is something positive, something we like or enjoy. Good also means:

PLEASANT   JOYFUL   WORTHY   RIGHT
HELPFUL   DEPENDABLE   JUST

We also said that maybe . . .

- **A good person thinks, says, and does good things.**
- **And a not-so-good person thinks, says, and does not-so-good things.**

But think about this: does a good person ever do bad things? Why would anyone want to do or say bad things? Why would anyone *not* want to show goodness to others?

Let's find out. In the list below, put a check mark beside any statement that is true for you. (And, hey—be honest! No one's going to tell on you for your answers.)

Check if you've ever:

- ☐ **talked back to your parents**
- ☐ **said something rude to your brother or sister**
- ☐ **wanted something someone else has**
- ☐ **disobeyed an adult**
- ☐ **said something hurtful to a friend**
- ☐ **took something that wasn't yours**
- ☐ **told a lie**

Want to know a secret? Come closer to the book. Closer. Closer.

Almost everyone has done all of those not-so-good things.

The truth is, everyone does wrong sometimes, even people we think of as "good." (And anyone can do good sometimes, even people we think of as "bad.") Why? Because it isn't easy to do good all the time. We can try, all on our own, but we will do wrong things.

So, how do we show **goodness** if we all do wrong things? Part of the answer can be found in our verse:

GOODNESS is the state or condition of being good.

. . . from the treasury of a good heart . . .

A TREASURY is a place to store money or wealth.

In other words, we need to put good things in our hearts so we can show goodness to others. So we can . . .

- be respectful to our parents
- be kind to our brothers or sisters
- be thankful for what we have
- be obedient
- be a loving friend
- be honest
- tell the truth

But **HOW** do we put good things in our hearts so we can show goodness?

If you're ready, keep on reading! (If you're not ready, come back tomorrow.) ★

DAY 2

HOW DOES GOD SHOW GOODNESS?
Psalm 119:68 and 2 Peter 1:3

Raise your hand if you totally understand the memory verse and how to put good things in your heart.

If not, don't worry. Let's solve this mystery right now. We need to get right to the source and talk about where goodness really comes from. Check this out:

> You are good, and what you do is good. Teach me your orders.
>
> **Psalm 119:68, NIrV**

The "you" in this verse isn't YOU as in the person reading this book. The "you" is God. GOD is good, and what *He* does is good—always.

God doesn't ever . . .

- lie
- treat people unfairly
- brag or boast to make Himself look better
- hold grudges or refuse to listen
- say hurtful or unkind things
- make a decision He later regrets
- talk about someone behind his or her back
- make up a story so He won't get in trouble (He never does anything to get Himself in trouble in the first place!)

God isn't like us. He isn't a good God who sometimes messes up. He is perfect, pure, and always right, 100% of the time. His goodness is on a whole other level—like the highest, most unreachable level in a video game. No matter how hard we might try to do good and be good, our goodness will never match God's goodness.

But here's the awesome thing. When we put our trust in God, His Spirit will grow goodness in us. When we need help to do good, the Holy Spirit helps us think of the right and good thing to do, and then He gives us the power to do it. Check it out:

> God's power has given us everything we need to lead a godly life. All of this has come to us because we know the God who chose us. He chose us because of his own glory and goodness.
>
> **2 Peter 1:3, NIrV**

That's good news, right? In fact, press pause to celebrate the fact that the King of the universe wants to grow His goodness in you. Go ahead and do your best power-up Fortnite dance. (Never heard of a Fortnite dance? Get an adult's permission to do an Internet search now!)

(WARNING: If you are in a public area with people around, you may get some strange looks. However, you should totally still dance it out!)

PAUSE
‖

Okay, okay. You can stop. But don't forget: God is good, and what He does is good. And the best part is, He wants to build goodness in us.

Remember when we talked about good things coming from a good heart and bad things coming from a bad heart? Here's a little math that might help.

$$\begin{array}{r} \textsf{YOUR HEART} \\ + \textsf{ GOD'S GOODNESS} \\ \hline \textsf{GOD'S GOODNESS IN YOU} \end{array}$$

God wants to fill your heart with His goodness so that you can do good to and for others. Why? Because that shows people His love. And the BEST way to make sure that happens is to do a regular heart check. At least once a day, you need to take a look at what's in your heart and ask God to help you remove anything that doesn't belong there.

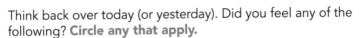

Think back over today (or yesterday). Did you feel any of the following? **Circle any that apply.**

bitter	envious	frustrated	spiteful
selfish	boastful	touchy	pushy
scornful	ready to argue	bratty	unforgiving

Did you circle anything? If so, did you feel that way because of something someone did? If that person were here right now, would you want to do good to that person? (Remember to be honest.)

Probably not! That's why a regular heart check is SO important. Because God wants to replace all that bad stuff—all that anger or frustration or envy—with His goodness. He wants you to have a good heart that produces good things instead of a bad heart that produces bad things.

So let's do a heart check right now. Write down anything that's bothering you. Then write a prayer to God asking Him to replace any bad feelings with His goodness—so you can clean that junk out of your heart. ★

DAY 3

HOW CAN GOODNESS POWER UP MY LIFE?
Ephesians 2:10

When's the last time something good happened to you?

_____

_____

_____

_____

How did that good thing make you feel? Circle all that are true:

In the space below, write the names of some of your friends.
(It's okay if you add your parents, coach, or small group leader.
Adults count, too!)

Now . . .

- Put a check mark beside anyone on that list who is kind to you.
- Put a smiley face beside anyone who is joyful (maybe they make you laugh a lot).
- Circle anyone who has been helpful to you (they've been there for you when you needed them).

Wow! You've got some quality friends. Did you know that God created you to do good to others, too? Check this out:

We are God's creation. He created us to belong to Christ Jesus. Now we can do good works. Long ago God prepared these works for us to do.

Ephesians 2:10, NIrV

Three KEY things to pay attention to here:

1. God made you.
2. When you put your faith (trust) in Jesus, God will work in you to do good.
3. God already knows the good things you will do.

Think for just a minute about your reputation. Your reputation is what people think about you based on what you say and do. Would you rather be known as a guy or girl who:

keeps his or her word	or	says one thing but does the opposite
puts others first	or	always pushes to the front
tells the truth	or	lies to get ahead

What if your classmates were given the same activity from earlier with your name on the list? Would they give you a check mark for kindness, a smiley face for bringing joy, or circle your name as someone who is helpful? How would someone else rate you when it comes to doing good?

Here's the thing. Once you understand that God is good and that He will help you to do good, you still have a responsibility to ACT. Goodness doesn't count for anything without action.

Keep checking your heart.
Keep asking God to "power up" the goodness in you.
And then get busy doing good.

Then you can build the kind of reputation that points others to God's goodness. ★

Before you go, let's practice our memory verse together. **Write as much of the verse as you can remember below.** I've given you a few hints. If you're stumped, flip back to page 147 to finish. (Don't forget to remind the adult you asked to do the same!)

"A _____ _____ produces

_____ things from the _____ of a

_____ _____ , and an

_____ _____ produces

_____ things from the _____ of an

_____ heart."

Matthew 12:35, NIrV

LOOK OUT!
A hazard to goodness is fear.

Have you ever gotten disconnected from a game you were playing and you didn't know if your progress saved or not? Talk about fear. You probably panicked a little. You maybe even yelled or slammed a door. When it comes to goodness, fear can make us freak out, too. It can lead us to do things we wouldn't normally do. Like we might not show goodness to certain people because we're afraid of what other people will think. Or we may make a bad choice because we're afraid to choose the right one; we're afraid we'll lose friends or lose something important to us. Don't forget that God wants us to show goodness all the time—even when we're afraid.

DAY 4

HOW DID PEOPLE IN
THE BIBLE SHOW GOODNESS?
Acts 9

Below are the names of some "bad guys," or villains, you may know from movies and games. **Draw a line connecting the correct villain to his or her game or movie.** (Pssst—the answers are at the bottom of page 163. But do the best you can without looking.)

Tom Nook	Super Mario Bros.
Dr. Robotnik (Eggman)	The Incredibles
Darth Vader	Angry Birds
Buddy Pine	Sonic the Hedgehog
Kingpin	Animal Crossing
Ursula	Star Wars
Giovanni Team Rocket	Donkey Kong
Prince Hans	Pokémon
Green Goblin	The Little Mermaid
Donkey Kong	Frozen
Bowser	Spider-Man

How'd you do? Did you recognize the names of the bad guys?

Well, here's another name to add to the list: **PAUL**.

But Paul is different from all the bad guys in the list above. For two reasons:

1. **Paul was a real guy who lived a long, long time ago.**
2. **Paul didn't stay a bad guy.**

We can read about Paul's story in the Bible. (We're just going to give you the highlights. But you should check it out for yourself in Acts 9. Just keep in mind that "Saul" and "Paul" are the same guy. People also called him Paul.)

We meet Paul before he discovered who Jesus really was. You see, Paul believed in God, but he didn't believe Jesus was God's Son. In fact, Paul's job was to hunt down people who followed Jesus and throw them in prison. Paul actually hurt people who loved Jesus. Pretty crazy, right? Talk about a bad guy.

But then something happened. Jesus spoke to Paul—out loud! Paul was walking along a road, and—just like that—Jesus started speaking. Jesus asked Paul why he was hurting people who loved Him. Right then, Paul knew he had been wrong; he knew that Jesus is God's Son. From then on, Paul's life changed. He stopped hunting Christians in order to throw them in prison. Instead, he started to tell everyone about Jesus.

But there was a problem. Not everyone believed Paul had changed. It would be like your parents waking up in the morning and acting like totally different people. Everything they did or said would be the complete opposite of everything they used to do and say. It would be weird, right?

Well, it was like that for Paul. He still had a bad reputation. Not everyone believed he had changed. That included Jesus' friends, the disciples.

Paul went to visit the disciples in Jerusalem. He wanted to join them in telling others about Jesus. But the disciples had heard about Paul. They knew of his horrible reputation. So when he came to visit, no one wanted to see him. First of all, they were afraid of Paul. Second, they didn't believe he truly loved Jesus.

Until a guy named Barnabas gave Paul a chance.

Barnabas was a disciple, too. He had heard what had happened to Paul and believed Paul had changed. So Barnabas went to his friends, the other disciples, and stood up for Paul. He told them they could trust Paul—that he was no longer a bad guy, but a Jesus-follower.

Because of the goodness Barnabas showed Paul, the other disciples accepted Paul into their group. Then, Paul . . .

> . . . stayed with the believers. He moved about freely in Jerusalem. He spoke boldly in the Lord's name.
>
> **Acts 9:28, NIrV**

Paul went on to lead an amazing life. He told lots of people about Jesus, and he even helped start some of the very first churches in the entire world! The history of the world was forever changed because of the good things God planned for Paul to do.

What would have happened if Barnabas hadn't shown goodness to Paul? Who knows? But aren't you glad he did?

Has anyone ever stood up for you? Were they there for you when no one else was? Did they help you through a really hard time? Who has shown you goodness like Barnabas did to Paul?

Bad Guys Answers:

Bowser	*Super Mario Bros.*
Tom Nook	*Animal Crossing*
Kingpin	*Angry Birds*
Dr. Robotnik (Eggman)	*Sonic the Hedgehog*
Giovanni Team Rocket	*Pokémon*
Donkey Kong	*Donkey Kong*
Ursula	*The Little Mermaid*
Prince Hans	*Frozen*
Green Goblin	*Spider-Man*
Darth Vader	*Star Wars*
Buddy Pine	*The Incredibles*

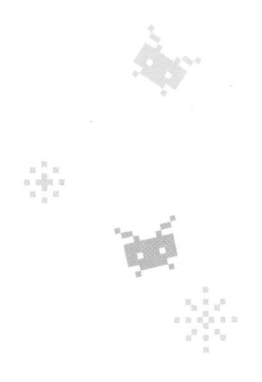

Then, if you can, do a video chat or text them and thank them for their goodness. ✗

Write that person's name here:

DAY 5

POWER UP
Matthew 5:14-16

Have you ever turned on a flashlight and shined the light in your own face? Or have you ever had your picture taken and the flash went off, causing you to see spots and stars and have to blink a bunch of times?

(Note: Do not shine a light in your face now. Or later. The light could damage your eyes. Seriously.)

Did you know that your life is kind of like a flashlight?

When we live our lives the way *we* want to, it's like shining a flashlight in our eyes. We can't see things clearly. We do and say things that we're not proud of.

But when we live our lives like *God* wants us to, we're like huge flashlights that shine our light outward. We can see better, and other people can see better, too. Check out what Jesus said:

"You are the light of the world. A town built on a hill can't be hidden. Also, people do not light a lamp and put it under a bowl. Instead, they put it on its stand. Then it gives light to everyone in the house. In the same way, let your light shine so others can see it. Then they will see the good things you do. And they will bring glory to your Father who is in heaven."

Matthew 5:14-16, NIrV

Look at the first word in that verse, "you." Now read the rest of the sentence. See? You're a light! Your life shines a light so people see something (or someone) more clearly. But who is that someone you help people see?

Look at the last two sentences: "'Then they will see the good things you do. And they will bring glory to your Father who is in heaven.'"

When you show goodness to others, they'll notice the good that you do. And that goodness with help them see God more clearly!

In other words, when your life is powered up with goodness, you shine the light of your life on God. It helps the world see God better!

Any time that you . . .

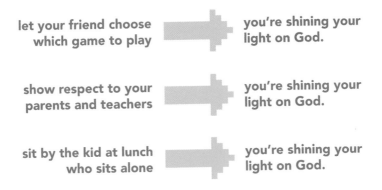

let your friend choose which game to play ➡ **you're shining your light on God.**

show respect to your parents and teachers ➡ **you're shining your light on God.**

sit by the kid at lunch who sits alone ➡ **you're shining your light on God.**

Now write down a few notes in each box on the next page. Spend a few minutes telling God you want to shine your light on Him and all He's done for you. ★

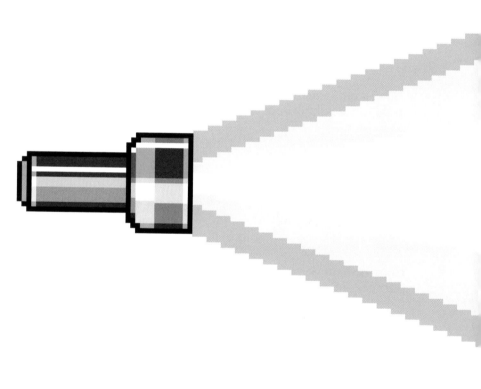

THANK GOD FOR SOMETHING GOOD IN YOUR LIFE

ASK GOD TO FORGIVE YOU FOR SOMETHING WRONG YOU'VE DONE

ASK GOD FOR HELP TO DO GOOD FOR SOMEONE ELSE

POWER UP CHALLENGE

Another week down! **What's one thing you learned about goodness this week?**

_____

_____

_____

_____

You know which question comes next!

Did your devotional partner memorize Matthew 12:35?

☐ YES   ☐ NO

X _____
(sign your name here)

Bonus: What did you give your partner for memorizing the verse?

_____

Now for your own personal Power Up Challenge.

Close out this week by doing something good for someone. Fill in the blanks below to create a game plan. If you can't think of anything, ask a parent for help.

WHO
(Who can I show goodness to?)

_____

_____

WHEN
(When can I show goodness to them? Pick a date and time.)

_____

_____

HOW
(How can I show goodness to them? You can choose more than one way.)

_____

_____ ★

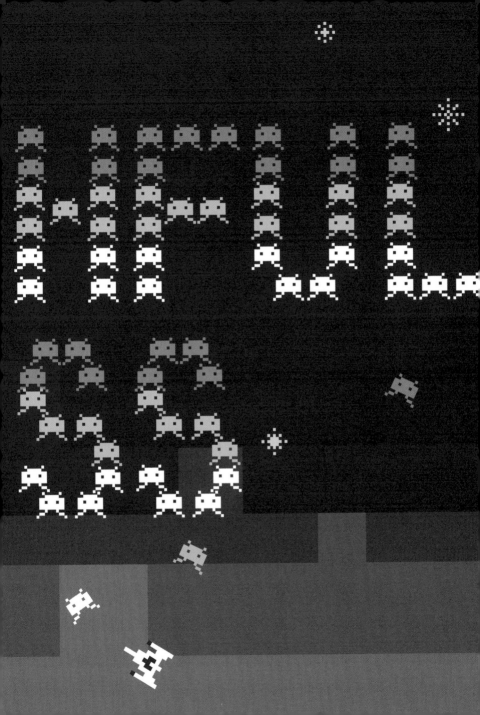

WEEK 7

FAITHFULNESS

Circle any of the following that you have done:

- flown on an airplane
- ridden a roller coaster
- been a passenger in a car
- sat down in a chair
- turned on a light

How many did you circle? _____

Did you know that doing all of those things requires faith?

Faith is trusting in something or someone. Think about it. To do those things, you had to have faith that . . .

- the plane you were on could fly
- the roller coaster you rode would stay on the track
- the car you were in would stop when it was supposed to
- the chair you used would hold you up
- the light switch you flipped would work

You put your faith in things, places, and people every day without even thinking about it.

To put it another way:

> Faith is being sure of what we hope for.
> It is being sure of what we do not see.
>
> **Hebrews 11:1, NIrV**

(Bet you know what's coming next.)

This verse is the **Memory Verse Challenge** for the week. Take a minute to write it somewhere so you can practice it. While you're at it, remind the adult you chose as a partner that he or she has a new verse to memorize.

Faith simply means to trust. So now that we've defined faith, what do you think faithfulness means? **Write your own definition in the space below:**

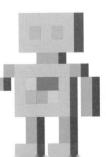

Pro Tip #16:

No matter how portable your Nintendo Switch is, it's never a good idea to play it while riding a roller coaster.

DAY 1

WHAT IS FAITHFULNESS?
Hebrews 11:1

Grab this book and your Bible and head outside. Go ahead.
I'll wait.

Now that you're outside, what do you see? Trees? Birds? Your
dog? **List a few things here:**

Who made that tree? Who gave that bird those super-awesome
aerodynamic wings so it can fly? Who gave you eyes to see, a
nose to smell, and ears to hear all those amazing things?

Yes! God did. He gives us what we need to live, like food and
air. He gives us good things to enjoy, like the warm sunshine,
shade trees, and best friends. But that's not all. God met our
greatest need when He sent His only Son, Jesus, to be our
Savior and to make it possible to be close with God. All of these
things that God provides for us are proof that He is dependable.

That's why we can have faith in Him, and that's why He wants to
"grow" faithfulness in us.

So, let's break down that word together.

FAITH + FUL + NESS = ?

We know . . .

FAITH = TRUSTING OR BELIEVING

**FULL = VERY, COMPLETELY,
OR CONTAINING AS MUCH AS POSSIBLE**

NESS = STATE OR CONDITION

Faith means to trust or believe.

Faithfulness means to be full of faith—to put your full and continuing trust in something.

Okay, are you still outside? If so, take a minute to look up at the clouds. What shapes do you see?

Draw one in the space below.

Now close your eyes and count to 100. Again, I'll wait.

Did you count ALL the way to 100? Look at the sky again and see if you can find that cloud. Can you? Is it still the same shape? Probably not. Why? Because clouds are constantly moving and changing.

Here's some great news. God isn't like those clouds. Because God is the same yesterday, today, and forever. He has always been exactly who He is—completely loving and kind and patient and good. Nothing you do can change who God is. He is steady and worthy of your trust. You can depend on Him. Always.

Just like you depend on a chair to hold you when you sit in it, God wants you to place all your trust in Him. We show our faithfulness to God when we continue to trust Him.

Even when . . .

- we feel like we don't fit in
- our parents keep arguing
- money is running out
- our pet runs away
- we have to go to a new school

That's faithfulness: continuing to trust in God. No matter what.

Write God a note telling Him that you want to be faithful to Him. Tell Him you want to show faithfulness no matter what's happening in your life.

DAY 2

HOW DOES GOD SHOW FAITHFULNESS?
Romans 8:38-39

What's the last awesome thing you did? Did you finally beat the high score on your favorite video game or app? Did you do something super-nice for someone without them having to ask? Did you totally kill that test everybody was worried about? **Write about it here:**

_____

_____

_____

_____

As many awesome things as you have done, there are probably a few things you've done that you'd like to forget. (We talked about a few of them last week, remember?) Don't worry. You don't have to write those things here. But take a minute and think about it. Have you ever:

- talked about a friend behind his or her back?
- made fun of someone?
- cheated on a test?
- lied to your parents?

Lots of people can say yes to those questions. But that doesn't matter; they're still not-so-awesome choices. There's another word for those kinds of choices—for the things we do and say that are wrong. Sin.

How do you think God feels when we sin? Angry? Disappointed? Sad? Maybe. But do you think our sin makes God love us any less? Check out what Paul wrote in the book of Romans.

> I am absolutely sure that not even death or life can separate us from God's love. Not even angels or demons, the present or the future, or any powers can separate us. Not even the highest places or the lowest, or anything else in all creation can separate us. Nothing at all can ever separate us from God's love. That's because of what Christ Jesus our Lord has done.
>
> **Romans 8:38-39, NIrV**

Look at that second-to-last sentence: "Nothing at all can ever separate us from God's love."

Nothing. Do you know how much nothing is?

ZIP.

ZILCH.

ZERO.

NADA.

NONE.

NO THING.

Nothing (not even our sin) can make God love us less. When you . . .

- start arguments with your sister
- punch your brother
- yell at your mom
- lie to your teacher
- say something bad about your friend

. . . God loves you. Period. You can't do anything to make God love you more. You can't do anything to make God love you less. God is the best example of faithfulness. He continues to love and support you no matter what.

In fact, God did something for you that shows how true and trustworthy and loving He is. Something that no one else could ever do for you. Do you know what it is? (Flip back to page 179 and re-read the last sentence in the Bible verses.)

That's right—God sent Jesus to be your Savior. The truth about our sin is that it separates us from God. But because God's love is SO big, He made a way to fix that separation by sending Jesus. Nothing can separate you from God's love BECAUSE of what Jesus did for you. Jesus died on the cross and took the punishment for all our sin. When we ask Him to forgive us and be our Savior, He will.

That's pretty cool news, right? Celebrate by giving God a virtual high five. Go for it, now!

VIRTUAL HIGH FIVE IN PROGRESS

The forgiveness that God offers us erases our sin. It's like our sin is completely covered up by His faithfulness to us!

In the space below, cover up the word SIN with the word
FAITHFULNESS. Use colored pencils or markers so there's
no trace of SIN left! ★

DAY 3

HOW CAN FAITHFULNESS POWER UP MY LIFE?
Psalm 46:1-3

There are all kinds of ways to stay safe when you're gaming.

**In Minecraft, you can build a fence
or wall around your house.**

**In Animal Crossing: New Leaf, you can catch
bees in a net before they sting you.**

**In Fortnite, you can build some extra-tall stairs
so you can better see your enemies.**

We have ways to stay safe in real life, too.

**Seatbelts
Smoke detectors
Life jackets**

I bet you can think of lots of other things and people who keep us safe. Name a few here:

_____

_____

_____

But did you know that we can find safety in something else? In someone else? In Psalm 46, we read this . . .

> God is our place of safety. He gives us strength. He is always there to help us in times of trouble.
>
> The earth may fall apart. The mountains may fall into the middle of the sea. But we will not be afraid.
>
> The waters of the sea may roar and foam. The mountains may shake when the waters rise. But we will not be afraid.
>
> **Psalm 46:1-3, NIrV**

Rewrite that first sentence from the verse here:

So, God is our place of safety. But how exactly *is* He our place of safety, especially since we can't see Him?

Read the following examples. Draw a line from each hard situation (on the left) to a way you can remember God's faithfulness (on the right). (Tip: There might be more than one answer for each hard situation.) What other hard situations can you think of to add to the list?

HARD SITUATIONS

When a friend hurts your feelings ●

When your dad loses his job ●

When you don't make the team ●

When your parents get divorced ●

When it feels like you have no friends ●

_____ ●

_____ ●

_____ ●

_____ ●

_____ ●

WAYS TO REMEMBER GOD'S FAITHFULNESS

● Talk to God and ask for His help

● Talk to your parents

● Ask your small group to pray for you

● Invite a friend over to cheer you up

● Talk to your small group leader

● Make a list of at least three things you are grateful for

● Ask your small group leader to help you find Bible verses to read

● Do something kind for someone else

● Remember the Holy Spirit is there to help you

● Think of a Bible verse that is encouraging

Everyone has times of trouble. That's just part of life. But those are the times when it can be hard to be faithful—to continue to put our trust in God.

That's why it's important to remember that you don't face hard situations on your own; God is there to help. He helps by putting people in your life to love and care for you and give you good advice. He helps through the Bible, which can remind you of all the good things He's done for you. He helps by giving you the Holy Spirit, who guides and comforts you through the hard stuff.

God is always with you, ready to listen and ready to give you strength. He wants you to ask for His help—even when you don't know what to say or you aren't sure He's there. Just talk to Him about how you're feeling. He can help you power up with faithfulness.

I don't know about you, but that kind of safety sounds like the best power up EVER. ★

LOOK OUT!

A hazard to faithfulness is being fooled by things that go wrong.

Have you ever been to a funhouse and looked in one of those wavy mirrors? They fool you by making you look taller or shorter or wider or smaller than you really are. Our lives can be like that, too. When things go wrong, we might be fooled into thinking that God has stopped caring for us. In other words, it's hard to show faithfulness when we focus on the things that have gone wrong. But when we remember all that God has done for us, we see things more clearly

DAY 4

HOW DID PEOPLE IN THE BIBLE SHOW FAITHFULNESS?
Acts 12:1-19

What do you think is the worst punishment ever? Rank the following punishments from 1 to 5, 1 being the worst one.

_____ **Being yelled at**

_____ **Losing privileges**

_____ **Getting grounded**

_____ **Being ignored**

_____ **Having a "time out"**

When Jesus lived on earth, He had a bunch of people He hung around with. He had friends—just like you and I have friends. Jesus' closest friends are called the disciples.

One of those friends was Peter. Peter got one of the worst punishments a person can get. Peter was put in jail.

Only Peter hadn't done anything wrong.

After Jesus died on the cross, He rose from the dead—proving He was God's Son. But not everyone believed that. A lot of people got angry when Jesus' disciples told others about the strange and wonderful things Jesus had done.

But Jesus' disciples were faithful. They believed in Jesus and told others about Him, even when it was hard. Even when they could be arrested for it!

That's what got Peter sent to jail: he was punished for his faithfulness to Jesus. Not only that, but the guy who put Peter in jail wanted Peter (and the other Christians) to suffer.

But then something cool happened. Actually, if there were a word that's cooler than cool, it would be that word.

Here's what Luke said about what happened to Peter while he was in jail:

> Peter was sleeping between two soldiers. Two chains held him there. Lookouts stood guard at the entrance. Suddenly an angel of the Lord appeared. A light shone in the prison cell. The angel struck Peter on his side. Peter woke up. "Quick!" the angel said. "Get up!" The chains fell off Peter's wrists.
>
> Acts 12:6b-7, NIrV

I mean, the Bible has some pretty amazing stories, but this one is crazy cool. (Tip: You should go read the whole thing when you finish reading this. Flip to Acts 12 and check it out.)

Imagine that you're Peter, sitting in jail for being a faithful Jesus-follower. You fall asleep between two guards, with no hope of being free again. Then, all of a sudden, an angel from God pokes you in the side and tells you to get up.

Draw how you would have felt if you had been Peter.

Peter's faithfulness may have gotten him thrown in jail, but it was God's faithfulness that got Peter out.

You probably don't have to worry about getting in trouble for your faith. But there are people around the world who are concerned about that. In some parts of the world, people are forced to say they have faith in things and people that they don't really have faith in. If they are honest about their faith, they could get put in jail like Peter. Or worse.

If you had lived during Peter's time, and you had been a Jesus-follower, how could you have encouraged him while he was in jail? **Below, write Peter a quick note.** Tell him how important it is to remain faithful, even when it's hard. ★

Dear
Peter,

Signed,

DAY 5

POWER UP
Matthew 28:20b

The human brain is a powerful thing. Yeah, it may kind of gross you out to think about what it looks like. But when you think about what the brain can actually do, it's mind-blowing!

The human brain . . .

- Can generate 23 watts of power when it's awake

- Contains 10,000 miles of blood vessels

- Can process an image that your eyes have seen for as few as 13 milliseconds

Our brains tell our hearts when to beat and our legs when to walk. They tell our fingers when to press the "A" button repeatedly in order to avoid oncoming danger in our favorite video game.

But one of the coolest things about our brains is their ability to memorize things. Think about it: what would our lives be like if we never remembered anything? Try waking up every morning and introducing yourself to your family over and over again. You may be nicer to your little sister because you forget that she poured juice on your tablet, but it'd definitely get old.

Our memories help us in ways that we don't even realize.

Hold this page up to a mirror to discover the following amazing ways your memory helps you:

- We remember that hot water stings, so we make sure it's a safe temperature before touching it.

- We remember that crossing a street is dangerous, so we look both ways before crossing.

- We remember that eating dog food makes us sick, so we eat people food instead. (Okay, maybe we just remember that we know dog food makes us sick. Hopefully you haven't tested out that theory!)

But there's something else we can remember that can help us in important ways: **God's words.**

When we memorize God's words, it helps us remember His faithfulness to us. Read this out loud:

> And you can be sure that I am always with you, to the very end.
>
> **Matthew 28:20b, NIrV**

When is God with us? Until the very end. The end of the day. The end of the test. The end of anything hard we must face.

Memorizing Scripture like this can power up our lives when it's super-hard to be faithful. When we're sad, worried, or upset, the Holy Spirit can remind us of a verse we memorized to help us feel better.

Grab your Bible or open up your Bible app. **Look up the following Scriptures and choose one. Then write it below.**

Verses to choose from:

Deuteronomy 31:8

Psalm 46:1-3

Psalm 119:105

Matthew 28:20b

Romans 8:38-39

Memorizing Scripture about God's faithfulness will power up our lives in ways we can't even imagine. ★

POWER UP CHALLENGE

Can you believe you're almost finished? Only two more weeks to go!

Did your partner memorize Hebrews 11:1?

☐ YES   ☐ NO

X _____

(sign your name here)

Bonus: What did you give him or her for memorizing the verse?

_____

NOW IT'S
TIME FOR YOUR OWN
PERSONAL POWER UP
CHALLENGE.

Take the verse you chose on Day 5 and write it again in a super-creative way. You can . . .

- use chalk on your sidewalk.
- finger paint on poster board.
- pencil it on blank paper and add some cool shading.
- find a mirror you see daily and write on it with a dry-erase marker.
- glue yarn on a sheet of construction paper.
- write it on white paper with a white crayon, and then paint over it with watercolors to reveal it like a secret message!

Display your verse somewhere you can see it throughout your day. (This will help you memorize it.) ★

LEVEL EIGHT

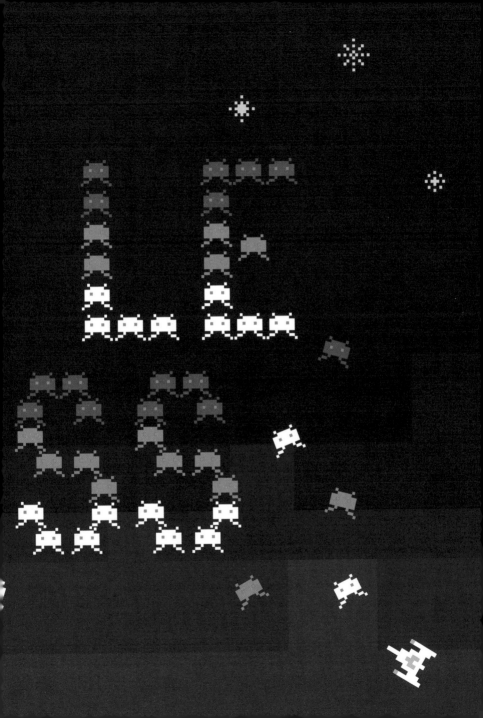

WEEK 8

GENTLENESS

Quick—what words come to mind when you think of the word "gentleness"? **Set a timer for 60 seconds, and write as many words as you can think of before the timer goes off:**

Maybe you wrote words like "quiet," "soft," "calm," or
maybe even "weak." If anything, gentleness may sound more
like a power *down* than a power *up*. And in a way, it's both.
Gentleness is powering up . . . by powering down.

Makes total sense, right? No? Well, check out the **Memory
Verse Challenge** for the week. (Don't forget to challenge your
adult devotional partner to memorize it!)

> Don't do anything only to get ahead. Don't do
> it because you are proud. Instead, be humble.
> Value others more than yourselves. None of you
> should look out just for your own good. Each of
> you should also look out for the good of others.
>
> **Philippians 2:3-4, NIrV**

These verses give us a hint about God's definition of gentleness.
(This probably won't be a surprise to you, but God's definition
might be different from yours.) As you read more this week,
you'll begin to realize it takes a lot of power and strength to
be gentle. ★

Pro Tip #17:
Being gentle with a skeleton
horseman will get you nowhere.

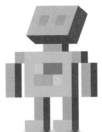

DAY 1

WHAT IS GENTLENESS?
Philippians 2:3-4

Have you ever seen someone take a picture while pretending to touch the top of a famous building like the Eiffel Tower? Or maybe pretending to hold up the Leaning Tower of Pisa? These pictures use something called forced perspective—a trick that makes our brains think that something is closer, farther away, bigger, or smaller than it really is.

Here's another crazy perspective trick called **Ninio's Extinction Illusion** . . .

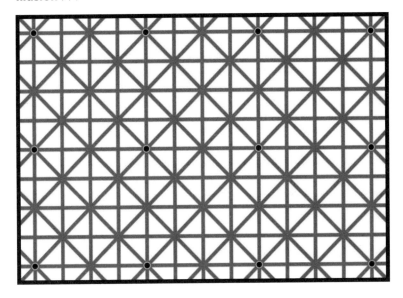

How many black dots can you see in this picture? _____

This image has twelve dots, but it's nearly impossible to see all of them at once. You may see three or four, but the moment you move your eyes, the dots you thought were there disappear.

NINIO'S EXTINCTION ILLUSION IS NAMED for the French scientist Jacques Ninio. You can read more about this illusion in his book *The Science of Illusions* (English translation: Cornell University Press, 2001) or by doing an online search of "Ninio's Extinction Illusion." (Be sure to get a parent's permission before doing an Internet search.)

There's all kinds of science explaining how our eyes and brains trick us into seeing (or not seeing) things. But instead of getting into details about *lateral inhibition* or *adjacent photoreceptors*, let's focus on one word: **perspective**.

Perspective is the way you see things. And everyone sees things differently. You have to be standing in exactly the right spot for it to really look like your friend is holding up the Leaning Tower of Pisa. If you're standing a little to the side, the illustion doesn't work.

But perspective isn't just about your eyes. It can also mean the way you see life. Depending on your perspective, a kid at school could seem super-cool or like a total bully. The dentist's office could be like a trip to an arcade or your worst nighare. Different people see life differently.

So what does that have to do with gentleness? In order to be gentle, you have to look at life from another person's perspective.

Maybe you want to scream and slam your door when your mom makes you clean your room before movie night. But when you look at it from her perspective, you see she's been cleaning the whole house to get ready for Grandma and Grandpa's visit this weekend. She really just needs you to do your part.

Or maybe you can't believe your friend uninvited you to his house. You'd been looking forward to spending the whole day on his Nintendo Switch. Now you'll be stuck at home with your baby sister who just wants to have a pretend tea party. But then you remember your friend's dad is finally coming home after 18 months of being overseas. Suddenly playing video games seems less important.

Gentleness is part of the fruit of the Holy Spirit, a result of the Holy Spirit guiding your thoughts, words, and actions. Gentleness means thinking about what other people need and then putting their needs first. It's going on the "baby" rides because you know your friend is afraid of heights. It's talking quietly in the library because you know others need to focus. It's fixing an extra sandwich for your brother because you know your mom needs to work. Remember the verses you challenged someone to memorize this week?

> Don't do anything only to get ahead. Don't do it because you are proud. Instead, be humble. Value others more than yourselves. None of you should look out just for your own good. Each of you should also look out for the good of others.
>
> **Philippians 2:3-4, NIrV**

Look at these verses again: "Value others more than yourself." "Look out for the good of others." That's gentleness. To be gentle, you have to learn to see things from a different perspective—from another person's perspective.

Write the following question on a scrap of paper:

WHAT DOES HE OR SHE NEED RIGHT NOW?

Tape that piece of paper somewhere you will see it every day to help you remember to look out for others. You never know; the question may come in handy next time you are tempted to be anything but gentle. ★

DAY 2

HOW DOES GOD SHOW GENTLENESS?
Philippians 2:5-8

In the game Minecraft, each player has an "inventory," a list of goods like food, building materials, armor, and potions. If Minecraft were real life, what things would you be sure to always have in your inventory? **Draw your real-life inventory below.** (Mine would be full of Doritos.)

Now, imagine playing Minecraft—in survival mode—and not using *any* of your completely full inventory. No armor. No tools. No materials. Nothing.

It may not make any sense to you, but that's what Jesus did when He came to earth. Remember this week's memory verse? Philippians 2:3-4? (Flip back to page 203 if you need help remembering it.) Here's what comes right after those verses.

> As you deal with one another, you should think and act as Jesus did. In his very nature he was God. Jesus was equal with God. But Jesus didn't take advantage of that fact. Instead, he made himself nothing. He did this by taking on the nature of a servant. He was made just like human beings. He appeared as a man. He was humble and obeyed God completely. He did this even though it led to his death. Even worse, he died on a cross!
>
> **Philippians 2:5-8, NIrV**

Do you get what these verses are saying? Jesus is God but He chose to come and be a human. He came here not only to save us, but so we could know what God is really like. (What better way for people to get to know God than for Him to come here as a person?) Sure, Jesus performed miracles to help others. But when it came time for Him to die on the cross so we could be saved, He went gently. He told His friend Peter that He could have called tens of thousands of angels to help Him, but He didn't.

Jesus chose to be gentle. He obeyed what God had asked Him to do—to lay down His life to rescue us. He chose to put our needs before His own. And that took a lot of strength.

CRUEL
means ready to
hurt others.

Jesus coming to earth as a Man and dying on a cross is a perfect picture of God's gentleness: He is strong, but He chose to serve us with His strength. Imagine if Jesus had come to earth and had chosen to use His strength like a **cruel**, hot-tempered king—forcing everyone to bow down and follow God.

How do you think people would see God?

How would your relationship with God be different?

As you think about who God is and why it's so astounding that He chooses to be gentle, read through the following words. **Draw a line through the words that don't describe gentleness.** Then, thank God for being all the words you didn't cross out. ★

SELFISH

RUDE

KIND

HARSH

PATIENT

STRONG

SHORT-TEMPERED

HUMBLE

LOVING

IMPULSIVE

CONTROLLING

FORGIVING

HARD

GREEDY

COMPASSIONATE

MERCIFUL

UNCARING

SYMPATHETIC

RESPECTFUL

UNDERSTANDING

IMPATIENT

DAY 3

HOW CAN GENTLENESS POWER UP MY LIFE?
Proverbs 15:1

Since the 1960s, scientists have been thinking up ways to prevent or stop hurricanes. Some of their ideas include:

- **wind farms**
- **dropping nuclear bombs on hurricanes**
- **spraying water-absorbing powder from planes**
- **making the surface of the ocean oily to stop seawater from evaporating**
- **creating a sonic boom in the middle of the storm**
- **shooting the hurricane with lasers**

But the most common idea or theory is cooling the temperature of the ocean. Hurricanes get their energy from warm ocean water. So scientists think if they can make the surface of the ocean cooler, hurricanes won't get as much energy. Then, when the storms hit land, they won't cause as much damage. But the question is: how do you cool an entire ocean? **In the space below, draw how you would cool the ocean.**

It would be amazing to slow down or stop big storms. But just as amazing, the Bible gives us tips for stopping the everyday storms in our lives. Like fights with your friends, scream-fests with your parents, or the silent treatment from your big brother. These are the kinds of storms that destroy relationships. Check out what Solomon wrote in the book of Proverbs:

> A gentle answer turns anger away. But mean words stir up anger.
>
> **Proverbs 15:1, NIrV**

Have you thought about the power words have? That when you choose gentle words, you can cool an angry temper? But when you don't, your words could stir up even bigger trouble?

Think of the last person who was angry with you. How does it feel when someone is angry with you? How does it feel to be angry with someone else?

It doesn't matter whether you are the one who's angry or the one someone is angry with. Anger hurts. It feels like a rock in your stomach or something burning in your chest. That's why it takes real strength to use calming words when you or someone else is boiling mad.

So where do gentle words come from when you're not feeling at all gentle? From God. His Spirit can guide you by helping you think of what to say (and not say) when gentle words are needed. The Spirit can remind you of Bible stories and verses that will help you speak more gently. He can remind you to ask Him for help in angry situations and will even pray for you when you don't know what to pray!

God wants to help you become gentle because gentle words help get rid of your *own* anger and help others get rid of *theirs*.

Think of gentleness as a giant laser beam. But instead of pointing it at a powerful hurricane, you can shoot it into the middle of someone's anger!

Complete the puzzle about times to use gentle words. Think about the gentleness that comes from the Holy Spirit—the gentleness Jesus showed. Then use the following clues to help you unscramble the underlined words. Write the unscrambled words in the puzzle blanks. ★

ACROSS

2. **orFiveg** when someone hurts your feelings.
3. Be the first to make up after an **artenmgu**.
6. **Agizelopo** when someone is angry with you.
7. **kAs** what is wrong when someone looks upset.

DOWN

1. **tnesiL** when someone needs to talk.
4. Do not **erteap** gossip (spread stories about someone).
5. Show **petcres** when someone has a different opinion.

Gentleness Crossword Puzzle Answers:

ACROSS	DOWN
2. forgive	1. listen
3. argument	4. repeat
6. apologize	5. respect
7. ask	

LOOK OUT!
A hazard to gentleness is selfishness.

Remember that squid-like Blooper in Mario Kart we talked about before that squirts black ink all over your screen and makes it hard for you to see everything around you? Selfishness—caring about you own needs more than others'—keeps you from seeing the needs of people around you. And when you can't see others' needs, when you are only thinking about yourself, it's impossible to be gentle.

DAY 4

HOW DID PEOPLE IN THE BIBLE SHOW GENTLENESS?
Mark 10:13-16

Let's think back for a minute. What kinds of games did you play when you were younger?

When you were a baby, you probably played with blocks. Or maybe you had a "blankey" that you slept with every night. Maybe you even had one of those fake phones that made noises when you pressed the buttons.

> **Pro Tip #18:**
>
> Pokémon is short for "pocket monster." (Not really a tip, but knowing this might make you sound smart in front of your Pokémon-obsessed friends.)

What about when you got a little older? Were you into board games? Puzzles? Maybe you played one of those educational video games where your favorite characters helped you learn how to add and subtract.

At the time, those toys were the greatest thing ever! But what about now? You're getting older, and maybe they don't seem quite so cool. You've probably donated them already, or passed them along to a younger sibling. Those games used to be your favorites. But now? Not so much.

It can almost be embarrassing to look back at things you used to like when you were younger. After all, there are so many new things you like. You've got new interests. You've got new skills. You want to play the latest and greatest games that all your friends are talking about.

When you hang out with your younger brothers, sisters, and cousins, you're probably not crazy about the idea of playing with "little kid" toys with them. But one thing's for certain—they feel like a million bucks when they get to play with YOU!

You know who wasn't embarrassed to be around little kids? Jesus. In fact, He loved it! Check out this example from the book of Mark.

People were bringing little children to Jesus. They wanted him to place his hands on them to bless them. But the disciples told them to stop. When Jesus saw this, he was angry. He said to his disciples, "Let the little children come to me. Don't keep them away. God's kingdom belongs to people like them. What I'm about to tell you is true. Anyone who will not receive God's kingdom like a little child will never enter it." Then he took the children in his arms. He placed his hands on them to bless them.

BLESS means to give or wish something good for another person.

Mark 10:13-16, NIrV

Okay, okay. Jesus again. But seriously, He is the greatest example of gentleness (and a lot of other stuff, too). If there was ever a person too important, too cool, or too busy to hang around a bunch of kids, it was Jesus. But that's not the way Jesus saw it. Jesus knew the little kids around Him were just as important as everyone else. He knew their needs mattered. And He knew that hanging around little kids didn't make Him any less powerful, any less . . . God.

Remember, it takes strength to be gentle. Talking with those children is exactly the kind of thing that made Jesus so strong.

How could you lead little kids in your family, school, church, or community with gentleness? For ideas, label each of these pictures with what each child might need.

The same is true for you. Playing with Hot Wheels with your little cousins isn't weak or lame. It's gentle. It's strong.

Gentleness is looking out for the younger kids in your school, reading to other kids at the library, making the new kid feel welcome in your class, or watching out for your little brother at church. It's knowing how to be a friend to everyone, no matter how old they are. ★

DAY 5

POWER UP
Titus 3:2

Circle the word in **bold** that make each sentence an example of gentleness.

My dad told me to go to my room, so I (**walked** or **stomped**) through the house and (**shut** or **slammed**) my door.

When my sister asked for the remote, I (**threw** or **handed**) it to her.

When I left the library I (**said** or **shouted**) goodbye to my friends.

As soon as I got home, I (**threw** or **set**) my bag on the floor and (**squeezed** or **rubbed**) my dog's fluffy head.

Gentleness isn't just about the words you say. It's not just about the way you hug someone or pet your dog. Gentleness is the way you *are*. Everything you do and say (even your thoughts) can be rough or gentle.

Sure, sometimes you need to scream or run or jump around like crazy. And that's fine—as long as it's not hurting or scaring someone else. God's gentleness is all about making sure other people feel safe around you. It means letting other people know you care about what they need.

The more time you spend with God, the more gentle you will become. The more you pray, read the Bible, and listen to God's Spirit, the more God's gentleness will be a part of who you are. Check out this verse from the book of Titus, where Paul was reminding God's people how to act:

> Tell them not to speak evil things against anyone. Remind them to live in peace. They must consider the needs of others. They must always be gentle toward everyone.
>
> **Titus 3:2, NIrV**

Always be gentle toward *everyone*?! Whoa. That's tough. You can't always be a totally calm, smiling, soft-spoken person. What about when you're hurt or stressed out? How are you supposed to be gentle toward everyone then?

The simple answer is: by spending time with God. Just like an apple grows bigger and juicier when it's connected to the tree, your gentleness grows stronger when you are connected to God.

To help you remember, write this week's memory verse on your bathroom mirror with a dry-erase marker. (Tip: Flip back to page 199 if you need help remembering it. Another tip: Be sure not to use a permanent marker!) You can write the whole verse or this phrase: "Look out for the good of others." Then, read the verse out loud each morning as a way to remind yourself to consider the needs of others throughout your day.

Write some ways you can show gentleness with:

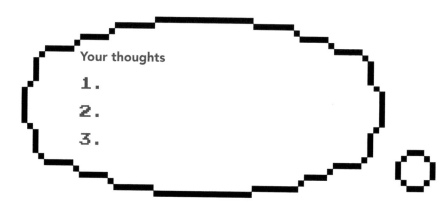

Your thoughts

1.

2.

3.

Your facial expressions

1.

2.

3.

Your touch

1.

2.

3.

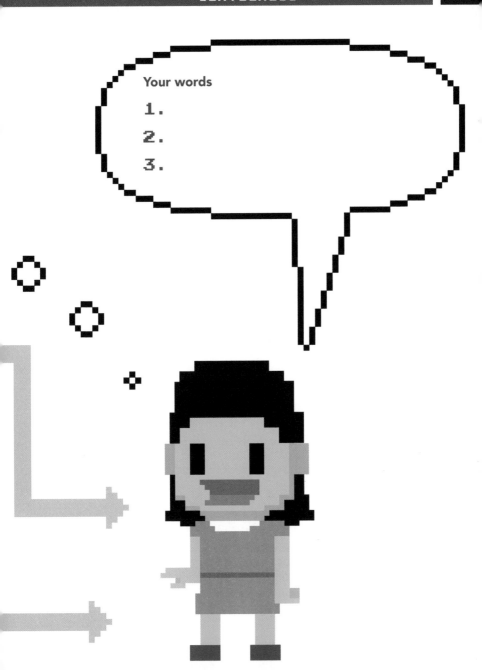

Your words

1.

2.

3.

POWER UP CHALLENEGE

It might be strange to think of gentleness as a power up. But as you learned this week, gentleness is actually a lot more powerful than anger or force. Before we get to this week's Power Up Challenge, answer these questions.

Did your adult devotional partner memorize Philippians 2:3-4?

☐ **YES**   ☐ **NO**

X _____

(sign your name here)

Bonus: What did you give him or her for memorizing the verses?

_____

Now, find that adult, a brother or sister, or a few friends to help you complete this challenge. Gather everyone around a table, or sit in a circle, and spend a few minutes saying the following sentences. Take turns saying each sentence in different tones of voice. Can you make each sentence sound gentle? Scary? Angry? Funny? Then discuss how the different tones of voice make you feel, and which way you would like your family and friends to talk to each other.

Sentences to say in different tones of voice:
- Please put away your clean clothes.
- What are we having for dinner?
- You can have as much cake as you want.
- How is your day going?
- There's a monkey on the roof. ★

BONUS CHALLENGE:

It pays to be super-gentle in some of our favorite games. Pick a night this week to have a family game night and practice gentleness by playing one of the following:

Jenga
Shuffleboard
Pick-up sticks
Bocce ball
Animal Upon Animal
Oh Snap!
Go Cuckoo
Tumble Tree

Don't Break the Ice
Shoot the Moon
Suspend
Junk Art
Toggle
Make a house of cards
Operation
Tugie

LEVEL NINE

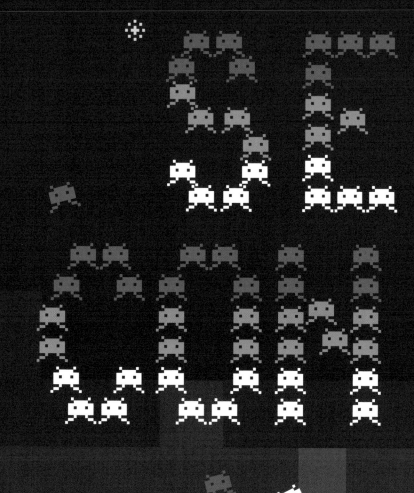

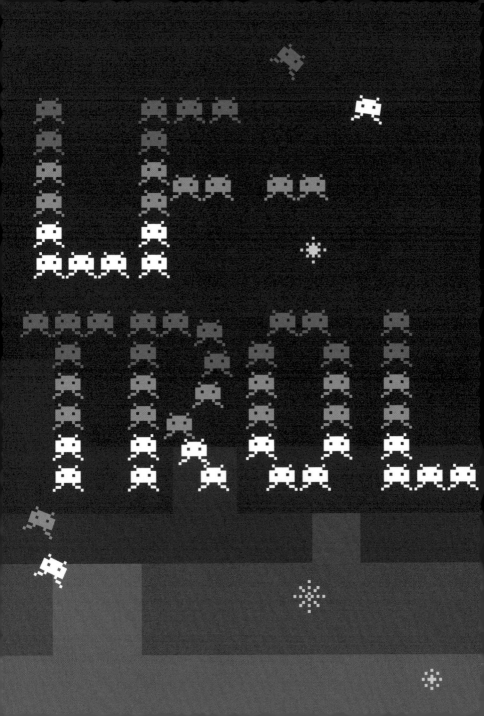

WEEK 9

SELF-CONTROL

If you've ever wondered why the fruit of the Spirit matters so much, you're not alone. Why be kind and loving and patient if you're a Christian (someone who has faith in Jesus)? Pretty much all Christians have wondered the same thing: If Jesus already took the punishment for my sin, why does it matter what I do? Think about this:

- Your doctor tells you to eat more veggies and less candy because she doesn't want you to get really sick.

- Your parents put limits on how long you can spend playing video games because they know video game addiction is real and dangerous.

- Your teacher asks you to practice sight words and multiplication tables because he knows an education will help you out in life.

- Jesus tells us what to do (or not do) because He knows the things that will make this life easier and happier.

To have a healthy body, we have to show self-control. To have a healthy mind, we have to show self-control. And to follow Jesus, we have to show self-control. We have to resist the things that tempt us to make poor choices. We have to make wise choices when it comes to things that *sound* good but really aren't good for us. (So maybe don't play twelve straight hours of Super Mario Bros. or chug an entire two-liter of grape Fanta).

Pro Tip #19:
Don't spill an entire two liters of grape soda
on your Switch while playing Mario Bros.

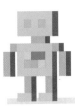

What do you think self-control is? By now you know it's part of
the fruit of the Spirit, but why is it so important?

_____

_____

_____

One last thing before you dive into learning about self-control
and how it can power up your life: your ninth and final **Memory
Verse Challenge**! Find your adult devotional partner and show
him or her this verse . . .

> Finally, my brothers and sisters, always think about
> what is true. Think about what is noble, right
> and pure. Think about what is lovely and worthy
> of respect. If anything is excellent or worthy
> of praise, think about those kinds of things.
>
> **Philippians 4:8, NIrV**

Okay, now turn the page! ★

DAY 1

WHAT IS SELF-CONTROL?
Philippians 4:8-9

Have you ever heard the phrase "you are what you eat"? **Draw a self-portrait of what you would look like if that phrase were true:**

Now, you know you will never turn into a Cheeto, no matter how many family-size bags you eat in one sitting. But what you eat does affect how happy and healthy you are. And that's what the phrase "you are what you eat" really means.

But what we eat isn't the only thing—or even the main thing—that causes us to be who we are.

You also are . . .

who you hang out with.

how you spend your time.

what you buy.

what you say.

what you think.

(Plus, you are your genes, of course.)

These things affect how happy and healthy you are. How good of a friend you are. How you deal with **disappointment**. How well you do what you need to do. And that's where self-control comes in. Self-control simply means choosing to do what you should do even when you don't want to.

DISAPPOINTMENT means feeling let down.

Pro Tip #20:

When you see a cute white dog in Minecraft, you should not pet it no matter how much you want to.

Look again at Paul's advice in his letter to the Philippians:

> **Finally, my brothers and sisters, always think about what is true. Think about what is noble, right and pure. Think about what is lovely and worthy of respect. If anything is excellent or worthy of praise, think about those kinds of things.**
>
> **Philippians 4:8, NIrV**

God knows there are plenty of things in this life that are out of your control. Things like where you live, if your parents get a divorce, or when someone dies. He knows life can be hard, no matter how much self-control you have. But He also knows that being in control of certain things will help.

Paul knew that self-control begins with controlling your thoughts, especially things that stay on your mind. If you think about something enough, it will start changing the way you act, the way you treat others, and the way you think of God and yourself. So why not try to think about good and pure things? Things that bring you peace. Things that please God.

Spend a few minutes coloring and decorating the phrase on the following page. As you make it your own, re-read and think about Paul's words. What things do you need to think about less? What things do you want to think about more? ★

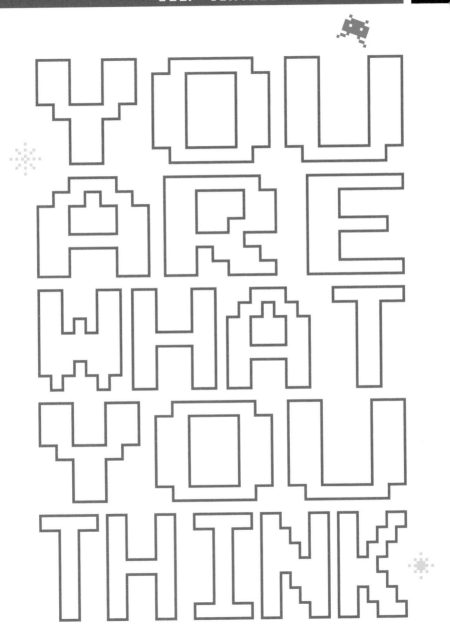

YOU ARE WHAT YOU THINK

DAY 2

HOW DOES GOD SHOW SELF-CONTROL?
Matthew 4:1-11

Why do you think God sent Jesus here to live as a human?

You probably wrote something like "to save us" or "to die on the cross" and you're right. That's one of the main reasons God sent Jesus: to take the punishment for our sin so we could be close to God. When Jesus died on a cross and came back to life, He made it possible for us to live with God forever in heaven. Whoop, whoop!

But Jesus did even more than that. When He came to earth as a human, we got to . . .

see God's power in Jesus' miracles,

hear and read God's words right out of His mouth,

and learn how to be the best humans we can be

. . . from someone who really understood what life as a human is like. It would be hard to trust, believe, and follow God if He had never lived here. If He had never felt what it's like to lose something or someone important. If He'd never had to make the right choice when it was really hard. If He had never been really tempted to do the wrong thing.

We can know God understands us fully because Jesus lived a fully human life.

Jesus is God. Completely. Fully. He never sinned. But Jesus was also human. Completely. Fully. Jesus got hungry, tired, angry, sad. Jesus was even tempted to do the wrong thing:

The Holy Spirit led Jesus into the desert. There the devil tempted him. After 40 days and 40 nights of going without eating, Jesus was hungry. The tempter came to him. He said, "If you are the Son of God, tell these stones to become bread."

Jesus answered, "It is written, 'Man must not live only on bread. He must also live on every word that comes from the mouth of God.'"

Then the devil took Jesus to the holy city. He had him stand on the highest point of the temple. "If you are the Son of God," he said, "throw yourself down. It is written, 'The Lord will command his angels to take good care of you. They will lift you up in their hands. Then you won't trip over a stone.'"

Jesus answered him, "It is also written, 'Do not test the Lord your God.'"

Finally, the devil took Jesus to a very high mountain. He showed him all the kingdoms of the world and their glory. "If you bow down and worship me," he said, "I will give you all this."

Jesus said to him, "Get away from me, Satan! It is written, 'Worship the Lord your God. He is the only one you should serve.'"

Then the devil left Jesus. Angels came and took care of him.

Matthew 4:1-11, NIrV

Sure, the things Jesus was tempted by might not be the same things that tempt you (except for the fresh, warm bread). But it's pretty powerful to know that Jesus really understands self-control. He knows how temptation works. He knows how hard it is to do the right thing. He also knows how good it feels to do the right thing.

How does it change things for you to know that Jesus was tempted—that Jesus had to show self-control, too?

Write your answer here:

_____

_____

_____

_____

If you were in the middle of nowhere, all alone, with no food for forty days, what might you be tempted by? **Answer by completing the following desert scene.** ★

DAY 3

HOW CAN SELF-CONTROL POWER UP MY LIFE?
James 3:2

In the game The Legend of Zelda, there is a weapon called the Master Sword. It's widely known as the most powerful weapon not only in The Legend of Zelda, but in any video game. It can **vanquish** evil. It lets you time travel. It is the surest way to defeat Ganondorf.

VANQUISH means to destroy or conquer.

Pro Tip #21:
Get the Master Sword.

If you could have a magical sword, what would it be able to do? **Draw that here.**

Great news! You have your very own "master sword." Okay, it may not be able to do all those things you drew, but it is powerful enough to change the direction of your life. And if you could control it, you would have some amazing powers. The problem is, it's really, really hard to control:

> Indeed, we all make many mistakes. For if we could control our tongues, we would be perfect and could also control ourselves in every other way.
>
> **James 3:2, NLT**

Our master swords are our tongues—the things we say. James says our words are like the bit that goes in a horse's mouth. He compares our words to the rudder on the back of a boat. He says our words are like a tiny spark that can burn down an entire forest. Our words determine our direction in life, the way our lives are going to go.

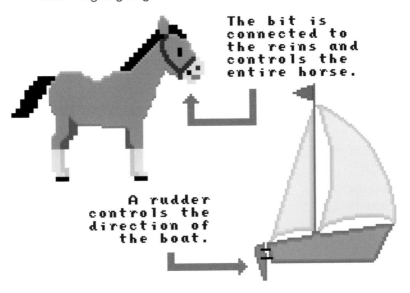

The bit is connected to the reins and controls the entire horse.

A rudder controls the direction of the boat.

Think about the things that our words can control. (**Circle every other letter in the following, starting with the second letter. Then write the circled letters in the blanks below.**)

1.

xmxaxkxexfxrxixexnxdxsxoxrxlxoxsxexfxrxixexnxdxsx

___ ___ ___ ___   ___ ___ ___ ___ ___ ___ ___   ___ ___

___ ___ ___ ___   ___ ___ ___ ___ ___ ___ ___

2.

xexaxrxnxpxrxixvxixlxexgxexsxoxrxgxextxuxsxixnxtxrxoxuxbxlxex

___ ___ ___ ___   ___ ___ ___ ___ ___ ___ ___ ___ ___ ___   ___ ___

___ ___ ___   ___ ___   ___ ___   ___ ___ ___ ___ ___ ___ ___

3.

xhxaxpxpxixnxexsxsxoxrxaxnxgxexrx

___ ___ ___ ___ ___ ___ ___ ___ ___   ___ ___   ___ ___ ___ ___ ___

Our words affect how well we make (and keep) friends. They can get us into trouble or steer us clear of it. They show whether we are liars, poor sports, selfish, trustworthy, kind, or fun to be around. Our words even affect attitudes and feelings—our own and others'.

The words you say (and the tone with which you speak) have the power to:

shame	hurt
inspire	heal
encourage	put down
bother	help

Our words are powerful. More powerful than we can imagine. If we could just control what we say, we would be able to control ourselves in every other way.

The problem is, none of us is able to control our tongues all the time. None of us *always* say the right thing or *never* say the wrong thing. (After all, we aren't perfect.) We need God's help. Remember, that's one reason Jesus sent His Holy Spirit to be with us: to teach us and guide us. So ask God to help you have more control over your words, and how you say them. You will have control over one of the most powerful tools in life. ★

LOOK OUT!
A hazard to self-control is impulsiveness.

That's a big word that means doing what feels good without thinking. Like racing your kart through a big shiny mystery box before realizing it's a fake! Next thing you know, you're flipped in the air and stopped in your tracks while everyone races past. When you do or say things without thinking, when you are impulsive, you lose control.

Word Control Answers:

1. Make friends or lose friends

2. Earn privileges or get us in trouble

3. Happiness or anger

DAY 4

HOW DID PEOPLE IN THE BIBLE SHOW SELF-CONTROL?
Matthew 26:47-54

The human body is weird and wonderful. It has dozens of reflexes, things it does to protect itself without you having to think about it. Things like yawning, blinking, or sneezing.

There are other things that, while possible to control, come so naturally they might as well be reflexes. Screaming when something scares you. Laughing when someone tickles you. Cutting off someone's ear when they try to arrest your friend.

Wait, what? Okay, that last example comes from one of the most powerful stories in the Bible. It happened when Jesus was in the garden with His friends, not long before He was killed.

While Jesus was still speaking, Judas arrived. He was one of the 12 disciples. A large crowd was with him. They were carrying swords and clubs. The chief priests and the elders of the people had sent them. Judas, who was going to hand Jesus over, had arranged a signal with them. "The one I kiss is the man," he said. "Arrest him." So Judas went to Jesus at once. He said, "Greetings, Rabbi!" And he kissed him.

Jesus replied, "Friend, do what you came to do."

Then the men stepped forward. They grabbed Jesus and arrested him. At that moment, one of Jesus' companions reached for his sword. He pulled it out and struck the slave of the high priest with it. He cut off the slave's ear.

> "Put your sword back in its place," Jesus said to him. "All who use the sword will die by the sword. Do you think I can't ask my Father for help? He would send an army of more than 70,000 angels right away. But then how would the Scriptures come true? They say it must happen in this way."
>
> **Matthew 26:47-54, NIrV**

Try to put yourself in Jesus' shoes (or sandals) for one minute. You are facing an angry mob of people. They are coming to arrest you, and you know they will kill you. You not only have weapons (like the one used to cut that guy's ear off), you also have the power of God Himself. All you have to do is say, "God, never mind. I don't want to do this. Send Your angels to help." And tens of thousands of angels would.

On a scale from "not much" to "Jesus," how much self-control do you think you could have in that situation?

Not Much   **Jesus**

It's hard to act like Jesus. He is *Jesus*, after all. But as we learned way back in week 3, Jesus did not *want* to die. He felt all the things you would feel if you were in His shoes. But He was so close to God (He *is* God) that He was able to have unbelievable self-control. And because of His self-control, we can have eternal life, in which all our sins are paid for and forgiven.

You may not ever have Jesus-level self-control, but the more attention you pay to His **Holy Spirit**, the more you'll be able to control your words and actions. Come back tomorrow for some tips on how to practice self-control. ★

Remember, the HOLY SPIRIT
guides and teaches us through
our thoughts. The Spirit
helps us remember or know
the right thing to do.

DAY 5

POWER UP
1 Corinthians 9:25-27

Do you have any goals? I'm sure you do. Check any of the following goals that you'd want to accomplish someday. Then, write a goal or two of your own that aren't on this list.

- [ ] **Play in the NFL**
- [ ] **Climb Mount Everest**
- [ ] **Write a bestselling novel**
- [ ] **Win an Oscar**
- [ ] **Win a singing competition on TV**
- [ ] **Dance in the Royal Ballet**
- [ ] **Perform on Broadway**
- [ ] **Own a record label**
- [ ] **Start a clothing line**
- [ ] **Become a famous chef**

My other goal(s):

_____

_____

There are two things pretty much all goals require: practice and commitment. The same thing is true about self-control. Mastering self-control can be just as difficult as climbing Mount Everest—maybe even more so! It's something you have to practice every single day.

Check out the way Paul wrote about self-control in his letter to the people of Corinth:

All athletes are **disciplined** in their training. They do it to win a prize that will fade away, but we do it for an eternal prize. So I run with purpose in every step. I am not just **shadowboxing**. I discipline my body like an athlete, training it to do what it should. Otherwise, I fear that after preaching to others I myself might be disqualified.

DISCIPLINED means in the habit of doing something, or ways of acting that come through practice.

SHADOWBOX means pretending to box with someone as a way to train.

1 Corinthians 9:25-27, NLT

Paul wrote about living a Christian life (with love, patience, kindness—all parts of the fruit of the Spirit) as if it's an event in the Olympics. He talks about training for it like a top athlete.

Have you ever seen or read about how top athletes train? Every second of their day is planned to help them improve:

- how much sleep they get
- the kind of food they eat
- how much water they drink
- what kind of exercises they do

Everything they do is focused on one thing: training their bodies to reach their goal.

What would it look like to treat your relationship with God like you were training for the Olympics? How would your daily life change if your main goal was to be as close to Jesus as any human ever? To be the very best you could possibly be at self-control?

Take a few minutes to write one way you can put the fruit of the Spirit into practice each day. (Some of your ideas may work for a few different things, and that's okay.)

Love _____

Joy _____

Peace _____

Patience _____

Kindness _____

Goodness _____

Faithfulness _____

Gentleness _____

Self-control _____

Just like love is the foundation of the fruit of the Spirit, it takes self-control to show all those other qualities of the fruit of the Spirit. It takes prayer, reading the Bible, learning about God, and even forgiving yourself when you sin. It takes the help of the Holy Spirit, every day. But just like winning a gold metal, the reward of living life full of the fruit of God's Holy Spirit is worth all the hard work. ★

Pro Tip #22:

Plan to read through this book again soon. (You'll probably learn some gaming skills you missed the first time around. Plus, powering up with God's Holy Spirit takes a lifetime of learning.)

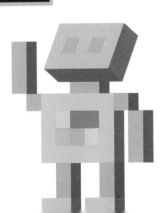

POWER UP CHALLENGE

This final Power Up Challenge is one that will take a few weeks to complete, but might just stick with you for the rest of your life.

But before we get to your final challenge: Did your devotional partner memorize Philippians 4:8-9?

☐ **YES**   ☐ **NO**

X _____

(sign your name here)

Bonus: What did you give him or her for memorizing the verse?

_____

Now, think of a good habit you want to get into. It could be completing your homework immediately after school. It could be putting your games away as soon as you're done with them. It could be brushing *and* flossing your teeth twice a day.

If you can't think of a good one, ask a friend or an adult for ideas. Then write your goal here:

I want to _____

_____

_____

_____

_____

They say it takes almost a month to form a habit. That's many days straight of doing something over and over before it becomes like a reflex. Thirty days straight before you don't even have to think about it. You just do it. Your challenge is to use the following chart (of 30 boxes) to keep track of your habit-forming progress. Over the next 30 days, use your Holy Spirit-level self-control to complete your goal every single day. **Start on a Sunday if you can. Then check or color in a box each time you pray before you eat, go for a walk or run, read a chapter of the Bible, or whatever habit you decided to form.**

Stick with it and it may just change your life! ★

Sun	Mon	Tue	Wed	Thu	Fri	Sat
1	2	3	4	5	6	7
8	9	10	11	12	13	14
15	16	17	18	19	20	21
22	23	24	25	26	27	28
29	30					

Love is patient, love is kind. It does not envy, it does not boast, it is not proud. It does not dishonor others, it is not self-seeking, it is not easily angered, it keeps no record of wrongs. Love does not delight in evil but rejoices with the truth. It always protects, always trusts, always hopes, always perseveres. Love never fails.

1 Corinthians 13:4-8a, NIV

Always be joyful. Never stop praying. Give thanks no matter what happens.

1 Thessalonians 5:16-18a, NIrV

Don't worry about anything; instead, pray about everything. Tell God what you need, and thank him for all he has done.

Philippians 4:6, NLT

Everyone should be quick to listen. But they should be slow to speak. They should be slow to get angry.

James 1:19, NIrV

Faith is being sure of what we hope for. It is being sure of what we do not see.

Hebrews 11:1, NIrV

You are God's chosen people. You are holy and dearly loved. So put on tender mercy and kindness as if they were your clothes. Don't be proud. Be gentle and patient.

Colossians 3:12, NIrV

A good person produces good things from the treasury of a good heart, and an evil person produces evil things from the treasury of an evil heart.

Matthew 12:35, NLT

Don't do anything only to get ahead. Don't do it because you are proud. Instead, be humble. Value others more than yourselves. None of you should look out just for your own good. Each of you should also look out for the good of others.

Philippians 2:3-4, NIrV

Finally, my brothers and sisters, always think about what is true. Think about what is noble, right and pure. Think about what is lovely and worthy of respect. If anything is excellent or worthy of praise, think about those kinds of things.

Philippians 4:8, NIrV